TEACHING CHILDREN HANDWRITING

*Historical, Developmental, and
Practical Aspects of Writing*

SECOND EDITION

by Audrey McAllen

RUDOLF STEINER COLLEGE PRESS

The publisher is grateful for the encouragement and support of Robert Dulaney in making this new edition possible.

The first edition of this book was published in 1977 under the title *Teaching Children to Write*.

Second edition, revised and expanded
© Copyright 2002 Rudolf Steiner College Press

Cover design: Claude Julien
Stegmann Hall photograph: Judie Bomgaars
Cover drawing: Aiona Anderson

ISBN 0-945803-55-9

Book orders may be made through Rudolf Steiner College Bookstore. Tel. 916-961-8729, FAX 916-961-3032.

Rudolf Steiner College Press
9200 Fair Oaks Boulevard
Fair Oaks, CA 95628, U.S.A.

To Ingun Schneider and Class Teachers at Waldorf (Steiner) schools worldwide

CALLIGRAPHY· BEAUTIFUL WRITING·
IS THE MOST DIRECT FORM OF
  ARTISTIC EXPRESSION· JUST AS EACH
    MOVEMENT OF THE DANCER IS
ABSOLUTE SO EVERY GESTURE OF
THE CALLIGRAPHER IS ESSENTIAL·
    IT IS NOT THE MEANING OF THE
CHARACTER BUT THE WRITING–THE
  MOVEMENT OF EXECUTION
        AND THE ACTION ITSELF –
THAT IS IMPORTANT· · · · *from the' Introduction by Tseng Yu-ho Ecketo, Chinése Calligraphy 1971*

Every sort of pedantry must be
kept at bay, if the art of education
is to have actual life. That depends
on making it into a real art, and
the teacher making himself into
an artist. And we in the Waldorf
School (Stuttgart) are able to
teach writing in an artistic way
with the result that reading can
be learnt afterwards as if it were
a matter of course. It comes rather
later than usual, but it comes as
if of itself.   *Rudolf Steiner lecturing at Oxford 1922*

Acknowledgements

I wish to thank:

The Editor of the Rudolf Steiner Nachlassverwaltung, Dornach, for permission to quote from the lectures of Rudolf Steiner, and the late Mr. Jesse Darrell for the translations of excerpts from lectures not yet published in English.

The editor of Thames & Hudson for permission to quote and reproduce illustrations from David Diringer's book *Writing: A Study of its Historical Development*.

The publishers Faber & Faber, Ltd., U.K., and Watson Guptill Publications, U.S.A., for the quotation from Alfred Fairbank's book *The Story of Handwriting*.

The publishers Godine, Noster, Non, distributor U.K.: Lund Humphries Publishers, Ltd., for the excerpt by Tseng Yu-ho Ecketo from the Introduction in *Chinese Calligraphy*.

The editor of the former Catfish Press, St. Ambrose College, Davenport, Iowa, for permission to quote from Edward M. Catich's work *The Origin of the Serif*.

The president of the Society of Scribes and Illuminators for the excerpt from *Writing and Civilization* by W. R. Lethaby.

Mrs. Margaret Frohlich, formerly of the Rudolf Steiner School in New York, for allowing me to quote from and to reproduce the alphabets in her book *Form Drawing*.

The librarians of Rudolf Steiner Library in London and of Gloucester County Library Service, U.K., for their help.

Many Waldorf teachers who sent me samples of the handwriting of their students.

Aiona Anderson for her artistic work on the cover and Erika Eikenboom for her detailed work on the lettering samples.

Judith Blatchford, Claude Julien, and Hallie Wootan of Rudolf Steiner College Press for their dedicated work on behalf of the new publication of this book. And warmest thanks to my editor, Ingun Schneider, who journeyed from California to go through the revised and extended manuscript of the 1977 edition. The context of words used in language today has subtly changed from the thought forms and connotations of the era in which I was absorbing language two generations ago. Mrs. Olive Tapp, now in New Zealand, typed the original manuscript for me. This new edition has become a forest of inserts through which Mrs. Schneider has had to wend her way. Both I and my readers will appreciate her original setting out of the Bibliography, and the References and Notes.

I trust that this book will be of value to teacher education programs throughout the world and helpful to teachers teaching the first three grades, especially.

Audrey McAllen

About the Author

Audrey McAllen has devoted her life to teaching in Waldorf (Steiner) schools, both as a class teacher and as a practicing teacher and lecturer in the area of special educational needs. In this field, she pioneered an approach, based on the principles of Waldorf education, for helping children with difficulties in writing, reading, and arithmetic; she has described these exercises in her book *The Extra Lesson*. As a result of her work, there is now a growing number of specialist teacher training centers around the world offering this approach in Australia, Germany, Holland, the United Kingdom, and the United States of America.

After her class teaching period, during which she had direct experience of teaching handwriting, Audrey McAllen undertook considerable personal research while developing her remedial work. This included participation in calligraphy courses with Ann Heckle, then teaching at the Art and Crafts Centre in Bath, England, and a wide-ranging study of the graphological aspects of handwriting.

Audrey McAllen's approach to teaching handwriting, as presented in this fully revised and updated edition, remains entirely consistent with recent mainstream research in the subject. It has much to offer to both new and experienced teachers, whether in Waldorf or mainstream education, and to parents who wish to become involved in this fascinating yet vital human capability.

Audrey has now retired from teaching and lecturing, but continues to offer advice and guidance to teachers and researchers from around the world. She lives in the Cotswold town of Stroud in Gloucestershire, England.

Ingun Schneider
Michaelmas 2000

Preface

When this book was first published in 1977, handwriting was considered in traditional education to be an adjunct to reading, and yet it was regarded, in the United Kingdom, as a subject to be taught in its own right. With present educational policies which stress early academic achievement, handwriting still remains a subsidiary skill to the attainment of reading. However, the concern over illegible writing and poor spelling, on the part of both examiners and the business community, is drawing more and more attention to this major deficiency.

North America, too, has an overwhelming number of children with dexterity problems. Unfortunately, the extensive use of computers in schools, often encouraged by gifts from companies, allows teachers an easy way out of dealing with handwriting difficulties and the consequent frustrations that these children have. The advocates of computer technology proclaim the demise of the necessity of handwriting, just as the introduction of television was expected to bring about a decline in reading. More perceptive observers point out, though, that no amount of mechanization will take the place of the ability to communicate through handwriting, even at the level of the simple handwritten note. The hand is, after all, the God-given tool for writing.

The main findings of my research in the first edition of this book, which was called *Teaching Children to Write*, related mainly to practical matters such as pencil grasp, sitting position, posture, and paper position, and the crucial area of the first seven years of a child's development, as seen from the perspective of educators following the approach of Rudolf Steiner. This completely revised edition contains additional contributions from the discipline of neuropsychology and its application in physical therapy and occupational therapy.

I have also examined the problems observed by calligraphers, teachers, and researchers such as Rosemary Sassoon and Jean Alsten who have designated areas of concern such as directionality, fatigue, and pain as considerable factors inhibiting the skills and fluency of handwriting. I find it so distressing to discover just how many children associate handwriting with pain. Professor Sassoon urges teachers to observe the difficulties of their students instead of blaming them for the deficiencies that they cannot eradicate on their own. In short, she encourages us to learn from our own students! I hope teachers begin to respond to this suggestion.

While preparing the second edition of this book, I was pleased to come across the title *Joining the ABC* by Charles Cripps and Robin Cox. The authors also give an historical survey of handwriting and its development in the twentieth century, and they, too, come to the conclusion that children should be taught a cursive hand from the start of their schooling. The book gives practical indications to teachers on how to help develop the required dexterity skills. In the Waldorf approach, the reader will find the qualitative aspect to their findings, and I hope this will encourage teachers in both Waldorf and traditional education to incorporate this necessary adjustment to the present indecisive way in which handwriting is taught.

I trust that the reasons for acquiring the specifically human skill of handwriting will become more apparent upon reading this book and that readers will see the advantage of pursuing further reading and research in this topic. One hopes that teachers and parents will then be able to relate more to the problems children are facing and find suggestions that will help them in the classroom. In this way, together, we may successfully reestablish the status of this unique human and social accomplishment.

Please note that the gender pronouns have been used interchangeably throughout the text. The terms "grade" (U.S.) and "class" (U.K.) are also used interchangeably, e.g. first grade or class one, or grade one.

Audrey McAllen
Stroud, Gloucestershire, U.K.
Michaelmas 2000

Preface to the First Edition

When I enquired at my local library about books on the teaching of handwriting, only the work of Marion Richardson and three excellent little instruction manuals published by Platignum were listed. The librarian told me that all the emphasis now was on reading and, therefore, so were all the books.

Surely this is symptomatic of our present situation. Reading difficulties have become so prevalent today just because we have put the cart before the horse. The young child is not given sufficient opportunity to write before he is faced with the printed page. This, from an historical development aspect, is quite out of step.

The capacity and desire to read actually only arises when we have something to write about. The very act of writing—the physical movements involved—prepares the body in large part for those subtle eye movements which have to be accomplished in a matter of split seconds during reading and absorption into consciousness. The movements required in reading are the fruits of the writing skill. Hence attention to detail and long practice of writing must come first, as reading from one's own writing goes a long way to reducing reading problems. Teachers who have worked in a Waldorf school recognize this from their own experience.

This book has been written principally for new class teachers in Waldorf schools in order to lessen the pressure of assimilating in a short time all the indications which Steiner gave on the teaching of writing. The teacher can then concentrate on reading the educational lecture cycles as a whole, instead of having to select from one and then another.

The book can also be of use to parents who wish to follow their children's work and, at the same time, to learn something about the fundamental principles of the education which they have chosen for their children. It may also be of interest to all other teachers who are deeply concerned about the problems that children are now having with regard to writing and reading.

All the practical examples described come from my experience as a class teacher and latterly from the remedial work which I have been doing with children who have difficulties in writing and reading.

The short study included in this book of the background indicated by Rudolf Steiner, will, I hope, also help teachers to realize the importance of the art of handwriting in human development.

Audrey McAllen
1977

Contents

INTRODUCTION TO WALDORF EDUCATION

The Aims of Waldorf Education

Waldorf education, known in the United Kingdom as Steiner Waldorf education, is now one of the world's largest educational movements. Its main purpose is to equip children with the forces to become fully developed people with the faculties to meet whatever life brings. Its aim is to ensure that students develop all their potentials, so that they will find the right place for themselves in the world. Through the development of moral stamina it is hoped that they will undertake a specific role in life because they feel that role to be necessary.

Students are educated to adapt and change readily to new conditions, an ever more essential faculty in the current global commercial climate. Hence a Waldorf education sets out to equip children to meet the demands of the modern world with thinking activity and perceptive feeling which, while recognizing conventional attitudes and stereotypes, allow them to meet the wide variety in people and life situations with confidence and inner freedom.

There are over 800 Waldorf schools throughout the world. Many countries provide government support to Waldorf schools. In the United Kingdom and the United States, the schools have to finance themselves entirely privately.

The Founding of Waldorf Education

The first school was founded in 1919 by Emil Molt, Director of the Waldorf Astoria Cigarette Factory in Stuttgart, Germany. Emil Molt wanted to offer a school to his workers which provided an education that would enable them to live in a spiritual or cultural life as well as in the prevailing business or economic life. This approach, he felt, would equip people to meet each other better as individuals with equality. While appreciative of this offer, the workers said they would rather have such a school for their children than for themselves.

Molt recognized that the teaching of Rudolf Steiner, called anthroposophy (consciousness of one's humanity), contained the genesis of such an impulse and therefore asked Steiner to become the educational director of the school. Steiner consented, with the proviso that he could select his own teachers, to which Emil Molt agreed, adding that he should have the right of dismissal if they failed to maintain the aims and standards of work at the school.

Steiner gathered twenty-four trainee teachers, who were already conversant with his philosophy and established in a variety of walks of life, and began an intensive training course with them from August 21 until September 6, 1919. The school opened on September 7, 1919, and by Steiner's death in 1925, the school was fully formed with thirteen classes educating children from five to eighteen years of age.

The Structure of a Waldorf School

Waldorf education falls into three natural stages which match the essential developmental phases in childhood described by Rudolf Steiner:

Stage One—The Kindergarten

The kindergarten is for children from age four to six years or so. No formal education is given here. The emphasis is on creative play in an environment which counteracts the disruptive, over-stimulating effects of modern technology and brings a more natural stimulus to the child's developing sense organs. Kindergarten teachers are expected to have such ideals that they are able to convey the moral qualities of goodness, truth, and gratitude to the children through storytelling and the rhythm of seasonal festivals. These qualities are the foundation for children to find, in their future schooling, that the world in which they live is both beautiful and deserving of their care.

Painting, singing games, and learning a foreign language through listening, speaking, singing, and playing all contribute to the kindergarten stage of education in a Waldorf school.

Stage Two—The Lower School

The lower school is for children from the age of about six and a half to fourteen years. The children now enter formal school. They meet their class teacher who will remain with them for the next eight years. The class teacher is concerned with all the problems of growth and learning which the children may have during this time, while the school doctor, if there is one available, with his additional training in anthroposophical medicine, will be responsible for the general health and wellbeing of all the children throughout their schooling.

The teacher's educational task is to present the subject matter at the time when it best complements the children's physiological and psychological development. When the subjects of the curriculum are taught in accord with the child's inner development, they have the power to enhance the child's faculties, skills, and abilities.

The Waldorf lower school (first through eighth grades) does not aim simply to teach children to retain factual knowledge to be reproduced on demand. Steiner felt that, in this age range, the child should assimilate what has to be learned primarily with feeling and should be fully engaged with warmth and enthusiasm for what is given. The lesson pattern in the lower school is therefore arranged as follows:

The first lesson of the day lasts for up to two hours with the children being taught by the class teacher. This is called the main lesson, and it covers subjects such as the three R's, history, geography, and science. Each of these subjects is taught individually in a block of daily lessons which can last for three to four weeks. The subject matter in the main lesson is presented artistically and imaginatively, and the children's involvement is maintained through movement, singing, and other activities which relate both to their own development and to the subject in hand.

After recess, which follows main lesson, the child meets other teachers for other subjects including foreign languages, music, gymnastics, games, and eurythmy. Eurythmy is an art of movement founded by Rudolf Steiner, adapted for use in education and in therapy. More recently it has begun to be used in business, due to its positive personal and social effects.

The afternoon lessons complement the main lesson and include painting, handwork, and craft subjects.

Stage Three—The High School

The high school educates students from fourteen to eighteen years of age. Here, students meet their specialist teachers who can enthuse them for knowledge in their subjects so that the desire for truth is engendered as a moral force. The curriculum is designed to introduce the student to a wide range of subjects which have intrinsic value as well as practical application. As with the lower school, the approach in the high school is to meet the student in his or her stage of growth, supporting the development of creative capacities, awakening responsibility toward the earth and humanity, and strengthening the will to carry through decisions.

There are three critical periods in adolescence. Around fourteen years of age, the young person is adjusting to high school, finding his or her way socially, drawing on newly awakened abstract thinking and judgment, establishing work habits, and challenging society to live up to its ideals. During the 16/17 year change, the young person is becoming more independent, is relying more on objective judgment, and is questioning the purpose of life. During the 18/19 year change, the focus is on the future as the young person is thinking about his or her place in society. This is a very important time in which strong forces of individuality and interest in the needs of the world should be cultivated and balanced. The Waldorf high school teachers adapt their subjects to meet the needs of adolescents during these critical times. The arts are integrated into academic subjects as well as having their own importance within the curriculum. While de-emphasizing formal testing, most Waldorf high schools offer their students opportunity to take examinations necessary for entrance into university. This differs from country to country.

Other Steiner-based Educational Establishments

This central educational impulse has led to the development of schools for children with developmental or physical disabilities. It has also initiated the worldwide Camphill Communities movement which provides homes, schools, and villages with sheltered work for those with special needs.

A Unique Approach: A Common Aim

Waldorf education shares with all other educational systems the desire for the greatest personal fulfillment for their students. Behind Waldorf education, however, there lies a unique philosophical perspective. Some of the indications from Rudolf Steiner may seem difficult, initially, for a conventionally secular Western world to absorb. The value of the educational approach needs, however, to be assessed through the manifestation of the education in the classroom, and in the consequent capabilities of the young people emerging from their Waldorf school life. Are these the qualities which we all—as a community of teachers, parents, and employers—desire for our children?

CHAPTER 1   •

THE RELATIONSHIP OF THE THREE DIMENSIONS OF SPACE TO THE GROWING CHILD

Who amongst us, on seeing an expanse of smooth, gleaming sand stretching out in front of us, has not felt the compulsion to run over it and to leave footprints embedded upon it? Does not the same desire also seize us when, waking on a winter morning, we find a velvety spread of snow covering the ground before us?

Open space calls up the impulse to move. Movement is the element that expresses most intimately our individuality through our will forces. This response to space through movement lies deep in our human make-up; it is a special phenomenon and needs to be recognized as such.

Drawing and Movement

As soon as a child can walk, one of his first impulses is to experience his movements in space and to leave his imprint in or upon it. He will find himself a stick to make a mark in the dust, and later, when he can grasp a pencil or crayon, he will start drawing a circle. Round and round he goes, until the center is reached and then out flies the line with a jerk across the paper! He makes another circle. Into the center he goes, producing what looks like a ball of wool, and then out flies his hand again. This is the first pattern he makes, later followed by swinging movements, side to side, up and down.

As his delight in what we kindly call drawings increases, these circling and pendulum lines gradually merge and become related to each other. A square forms, and suddenly we have the beginnings of a house before our eyes.

The paper which he has in front of him is, for him, a version of the ground upon which he walks. It has boundaries, though, which limit him from seeing the larger expansions in the drawing movements which he makes when he overshoots them. Nevertheless, he can place the paper on the floor and kneel on it, or put it on a chair and stand by it. It is a wonderful moving piece of ground over which he himself is in control. It is on this paper that the child exercises the sense of his own movements. The patterns of dots, the side to side, up and down pendulum movements, and the swirling loops are all educating his eye-hand coordination. This is an essential foundation for the development, later on, of handwriting skill.

Rhoda Kellogg, early childhood educator in the United States, suggests that a child's mind develops through the impact of his own scribbling and that, as he teaches himself to draw, he experiences his own motivation from within himself. As this scribbling is a spontaneous activity, it has meaning for further basic human capabilities. These include the integration of other capacities: the exercising of the intelligence and the critical operations in writing and reading. The pleasure associated with undisturbed scribbling can also extend into writing, despite its more restricted movements.[1]

Interference by adults who want him to do something specific, or who ask him questions about what he is doing, disrupts this process and disturbs his will forces. No wonder there is a yowl of rage when he is suddenly required to stop!

Boundaries: Above and Below, Forward and Backward

After the first static forms such as the circle, the square, and the triangle have been mastered, the next features to appear in his drawings are the boundaries of above and below, for example, a line of blue sky at the top of the paper and a line of green or brown at the bottom. Other scribbles, more meaningful for him than for us, still dance freely on the page. But the time comes when the house has found the site it stands on and an awareness of symmetry enters the drawing. Flowers appear on each side of the house, which is flanked left and right by a tree. Maybe there are two houses. . . .

The last stage of this growing awareness of space and his place in it is the ability to express the meaning of forward and backward. Just watch him make a rainbow shine over his house; watch him drawing the curve of its arc under which he can pass to and fro.

Now it is time for us to stop merely admiring his prowess as an artist and ask ourselves: What is he really doing? What is he showing us quite unconsciously in these first visual works of his? The objects, flowers, trees, lawns, and pathways can indeed be seen as reproductions of the essential structure of his own body, which he is able to feel through the craftsman's tools of the body: the hands, fingers, feet, and toes.

From Head to Foot

In his educational lectures,[2] Steiner tells us that he never once found a child's drawing of the objects of the sense world in which there was not expressed something of the child himself. Those first scribbles are part of the child's own physiological human mystery. The concentration, the movement, the triumph of completion is the *art* we should be admiring when the child places the piece of paper in front of us.

In the drawings of his house and garden, which come later, he is telling us of the adventure he is having of growing into his body. And what hard work it is for some children. What difficulties must they be encountering when, at around seven years, the house will stay lopsided, the tree continues to grow spindly and leafless, and the sky still refuses to meet with the earth?

These pictures are a map of the route each child is taking from his head to his feet in his first years of life on earth. So, when we want to encourage the expansion from drawing into writing, we must try not to break off abruptly the experience he is having of himself in relation to the pictures which he is making. If we do break the natural progression, we will most probably hinder his growth and sense of bodily well-being.

By imposing on him artificial restraints or concepts such as letter symbols, with which he does not yet have any connection, we will corrupt these natural forces of the will. These will forces still have their place in bodily functions like growth, healthy sleep and digestion, skillful handling of objects, walking with a free rhythmical swinging of the arms, balancing and jumping, and skipping joyfully along the road.[3]

If the growth into the bodily functions is disturbed or limited, then in the end, children may express themselves destructively. We find those who start messing up and scribbling over what they or their friends have done—a sure sign that there are problems already present for the educator to heal. We could do well to ponder the connection between the interruption of a very young child's organic development and his aversion, later, to school lessons.

So how can we come to a clear understanding of the child's development in relation to the faculties which he needs?

Powers of the Human Soul

Steiner describes to us how the human form is basically threefold in its physical structure: the head, center for the nervous system; the chest, center for the heart, breathing, and circulation; the limbs, center of the metabolic processes. These correspond to the inner soul functions of thinking, feeling, and the will. Integrating and directing these three is the ego or I, the guiding spiritual organ.

System	Function	Soul Process
Head	Center of nervous system	Thinking
Chest	Center for heart, circulation, breathing	Feeling
Limbs	Center for metabolic processes	Willing

It is important to remember in this context that the substances of which our body is composed, apart from a few specialist cells, are completely changed every seven years. It is the archetypal form of the physical body which is the constant factor. This form is the means by which the spirit incorporates itself into the evolutionary process.[4]

The three soul powers of thinking, feeling, and the will come to maturity as the first three seven-year developmental stages draw to a close at age twenty-one. Each stage culminates in a specific physiological development: the change of teeth, the arrival of puberty, and finally the integration associated with adulthood, once called the "coming of age."[5]

These fundamental observations (summarized below), which are, of course, visible to us all, form the basis of Rudolf Steiner's approach to educational psychology; yet they are largely overlooked by modern educators. The physical and psychological implications of this seemingly simple idea are fully explained in Steiner's lectures to teachers.[6] They may be summarized as follows:

From Birth to 7 years	The focus is on organic growth; Initially the totality of the physical body is a sense organ; The foundation of will is experienced through self-movement; Change of teeth takes place as this period comes to an end; The life/etheric forces are then freed from those of the mother's.
Latency Phase: 7 to 14 years	The rhythm of breathing and blood circulation harmonize to the adult ratio at around 9 years of age; The foundation for pictorial/feeling thinking develops.
Puberty: 14 to 21 years	Sexual maturity takes place; Abstract thinking and personal thinking develop; Soul/astral forces are freed from the life/ether body.
Integrated Adult: From 21 years	The ego ("I") directs the soul powers of thinking, feeling, willing, which are now freed from their organic function of growth.

Form and Space

Let us now consider the human form and its relation to the surrounding space, that is, to the possibilities of moving in space, of moving the limbs sideways, upward, downward, forward, and backward. Most people have a distinct perception of being "two-sided" and of each side's having different powers and functions. We know that we are right- and left-sided beings, rather than the symmetrical ones that a first glance suggests.

Closer inspection shows finer differentiation. The right side of the face has a distinctly different expression from that of the left side. Cover each side of a photograph consecutively and this becomes clearly apparent. The activities of left and right differ. The left arm protects and enfolds: the warrior's shield is slung on his left arm; the mother enfolds her baby with her left arm. The right arm wields the sword and is generally used for skilled movements. The soul that is not able to take up the archetypal pattern of left and right often finds himself at a serious disadvantage in the community.

Our body is also structured so that back and front, described spatially as forward and backward, are strictly differentiated. The senses and their activities are all directed forward: sight, taste, smell, touch; we even tend to bring our "best ear" towards the front when listening intently. Our sense of sight plays a significant role in our ability to maintain our balance.

What we look like from behind is hidden from us. Only concentrated inner imaginative attention can give us some idea of how we look from behind when we are walking. Try walking backwards in a large open space and discover how this draws together one's consciousness of self.

Above and below are also related to individual attitudes towards life and their spatial relationship. The person who walks holding his head upward or, conversely, with his head bent forward, is indicative of this. The movements of one's head have, of course, a freer relationship to the four directions of space as compared with the body below.

Spatial Development from Birth to Seven Years

From Birth to the Beginning of Speech

It is educationally important to recognize that the way the earliest spatial relationship of the body's development is brought to the child makes a difference. Our brain, in whatever civilization or epoch we have been born, has basically the same overall pattern.[7] In short, the brain is an archetypal structure, as is the structure of the whole body. Hence, initial sensory stimulation that the infant experiences calls on the particular areas of the brain related to the particular stimulation. Interestingly, recent research has shown that the Broca center does not have the dominant role for speech as was previously thought.[8]

Shortly after birth, the first experience of right and left is introduced to the newly arrived soul. His first experience of unity with the earth is through nourishment, which traditionally comes from the right and then from the left when he takes his first feed from his mother's breasts. When feeding from the right breast, his right arm is free; this moves and waves with the effort and enjoyment of feeding. When he is changed over to the other breast, his left arm is freed.

Now contrast this developmental experience with the process of bottle feeding. The mother is unaware of any need for differentiation and so uses the arm most convenient and comfortable for her. She would usually support her baby with her left arm and hold the bottle in her right hand. The baby's left arm would therefore have greater freedom to move and wave about.

This unequal stimulation of one side of the body for such a basic function immediately after birth, and continuing at regular intervals for four or five times a day during the first vital weeks of life, could possibly weaken the later developmental stage of ambidexterity (see chapter 7, pages 94-95, 99). Parents, noticing the tendency for use of the left side of the body, may then assume that their child is left-handed and make no attempt to intervene, in contrast to what was done until the 1920s or so. Recent research, however, shows that brain activity and growth go hand in hand: it is not only a question of "use it or lose it" but use it as much as you can.[9]

In addition to receiving nourishment, the newly arrived soul has to be introduced to a rhythmical pattern of sleep. Here the experienced nurse in the newborn nursery can make us aware of how the baby is brought to a natural experience of the human archetypal pattern of left and right by the correct wrapping of the baby for his time of sleep. She tucks his left arm first under the shawl and wraps it round him so that the right arm is over the left and thus is the one to be freed first if he wriggles to release himself. For weeks the baby lies on his back, then comes to the discovery that he can turn himself over on his own. As a result, he now experiences his weight from *in front*.

So it proceeds. He first experiences *forward* and *back* in the horizontal when he crawls and then learns to reverse! Finally the great moment arrives when the fully human experience takes place, the child lifts himself into three-dimensional space and experiences the sensation of *above*, *below*, *forward*, and *backward* from the vertical position which enables him to turn freely to the *left* and to the *right*, to jump *up* and *down*, and run to wheresoever he chooses.

In this way there are laid down those faculties by means of which one is later to develop a conscious mastery of space and, as a reflection of it, awareness of one's self. It is truly noteworthy that, along with this mastery of space experienced through the muscular system, the uniquely human capacity of speech develops.

From Speech to Writing

Thus is every human being occupied in the first eighteen months of life; each child also has an inner experience of this bodily developmental process. It is a deep and fundamental experience, and the child shows us how it has been taken up within his organism when he begins to objectify these bodily processes in the activity of drawing, as we have already described.

At first the house is merely an object anywhere on the paper. Then a little sky appears, followed by some indication of earth or grass. When the house is placed on this earth then a distinct development has arrived. This shows that the *above-below* relationship of space has been established, usually between the ages of four and five years. Consciousness of symmetry (*left-right*) develops later: a tree on either side of the house, flowers on each side of the path. Finally, when we see the arc of the rainbow appearing quite suddenly, we know that the recapitulation of the moment of the first standing on his feet and walking *forward* and *backward* has been reached.[10]

By now the owner of this dwelling will be in the picture. He should show us how he relates to the gift of the archetypal eternal form of the human being and how he has inserted his personal signature upon it. Ideally, he will show the threefold structure of his body, a round head, his chest and trunk delineated by a skirt or pants, and arms and legs with hands and feet.

The forms of the house—the triangle and square and the circling arch of the rainbow—have behind them the archetypal forms found in the natural world, in which he has lived in empathy for the first seven years of his life, and the forms of the structure (skeleton, muscles, nerves) of his body. Indeed, these were the basic forms of architecture until the beginning of the twentieth century.[11]

In these first six to seven years of life, the child's soul has completed its work of remolding the body inherited from his parents into one that belongs to him. All the physical matter he was born with has been expelled. The teeth, the densest concentration of substance, have begun to loosen. The child is ready for school. A new stage of consciousness is about to develop, one in which he will live in a feeling-pictorial way of expressing himself.[12]

Now is the time that he is ready to learn handwriting, a faculty for which he has been preparing himself from his earliest unformed scribblings.

Note: The neuropsychological development that I have described in the foregoing chapter is common to all children and is related to the attainment of skills. A description of the physical, constitutional, and soul development on which the individual's latent faculties (social development stages, innate gifts for music, numbers, language, etc.) depend can be found in such books as Bernard Lievegoed's *Phases of Childhood* and Joan Salter's *The Incarnating Child*.

CHAPTER 2

THE ALPHABET AND WRITING AS A PICTURE OF THE DEVELOPMENT OF HUMAN CONSCIOUSNESS

Writing, as we understand it, is a conscious activity and inseparably bound up with the development, comparatively recent, of man's conscious intellect.[1]
—David Diringer

When we approach the task of teaching children handwriting, it is useful to pause and consider the historical perspectives which lie behind the very possibility of this human activity. The developmental thresholds through which various cultures traveled in reaching the capability of handwriting, especially the consciousness required for such a conceptual capability, are so substantial that these must surely still have significance to the new generation of writers. There has been a great deal of research and writing about such matters. This chapter invites the reader to contemplate the philosophical implications around this activity, rather than the more practical aspects of handwriting which characterize the later chapters.

The quotation above is from David Diringer's life work on the sources of the alphabet and the development of writing. Dr. Diringer researched the symbols used by civilizations throughout the various historical epochs up to and including present-day agrarian societies.

From this research, he identified a critical moment in human evolution—the arrival of the human conscious intellect—and concluded that this was a comparatively recent development. It is interesting that Susan Greenfield in her book, *The Human Brain*, after describing all the knowledge we have now of its intricate functioning and development, comes to the question: Are we conscious?[2] After listing all the possible options, her suggestion is that consciousness grows and does not appear suddenly at any one particular stage of development.[3] Diringer also showed that the earliest forms of writing did not appear before the middle of the fourth millennium B.C.

If conscious intellectual development was not apparent until after this time, what kind of consciousness did the human being have prior to it? During the 1990s, the results of extensive research into the development of human consciousness have been published. We see in these descriptions the mirroring of specific spiritual realities which Rudolf Steiner had described at the beginning of the twentieth century. Steiner explained that, prior to around 3000 B.C., human beings were generally in possession of natural clairvoyance. He suggested that our ancestors had quite a different experience of the waking and sleeping states of consciousness from that which we have today.

The impressions made by the surrounding physical world were not so clear and exact, but had a similarity to the images we now have in dreams. However, in those times, when people slept, they retained their consciousness, and "spiritual beings" and their activities appeared to them. On waking, they remembered what they had experienced. This enabled them to recognize how the dreamlike impressions which they received from their senses when awake were the work of these same beings. As a result, our ancestors realized that the physical world in which they lived was produced by the creative activity of the spiritual beings whom they perceived in their sleep.[4]

Rudolf Steiner indicates approximately 3000 B.C. as the time when this mode of consciousness began to fade, to be replaced gradually by our present consciousness. Today's consciousness itself matured and became universal in the West from the last third of the nineteenth century. Is it not remarkable that it was about this time that the demand arose for universal literacy?

As the natural clairvoyance gradually decreased, people's power of memory was enhanced, not only memory of events of their own lives, but also of the lives of their ancestors. These faculties also ebbed away as the human sense organism responded to the world around; now memory had to be stimulated from outside. Buildings of antiquity expressed this need for external memory stimulus. Biblical examples include Jacob's erection of a stone to recall his vision at Bethel, and the twelve stones from the River Jordan set up at Joshua's command as a reminder to the children of Israel of the parting of the river's waters to provide them with a safe, dry passage. A reminder of this type of memory must have been stirred in the national subconscious when it was decided in many towns to erect a cenotaph pillar to keep alive the memory of those killed in the First World War.

However, in the religious centers of early times, certain human beings retained the old type of consciousness and memory, and they were singled out to undergo training of these faculties. They were sent from these centers to travel the countryside to tell the people, who had lost their direct connection with the spiritual world, how the work of higher beings was involved in human life. Many of these experiences are the basis of what are for us today the great myths and sagas. Others became the stories told around the hearth fire in winter and were thus passed down from generation to generation. They lingered on among country people until the nineteenth century, to be collected and to become part of our cultural heritage through the printed page.

Although covered but briefly here, the historical sequence described by Rudolf Steiner and others leads to the conclusion that there has been a specific cycle of development in human capability: from direct experience, to memory,[5] speech, writing, and finally, reading.

Direct Experience

Memory

Speech

Writing

Reading

Awareness of this sequence can have a profound influence on the way we plan the teaching of the skills of both writing and reading.

The Development of Writing

Reverence for Writing

How did ancient people regard writing? Diringer tells us that, in all ancient cultures, writing was held in awe and its invention was frequently attributed to divinities or folk heroes. Modern consciousness, of course, may smile at this, but we should consider this as having scientific validity when viewed from the perspective of human spiritual historical development.[6]

The reverence for the art of writing came from the recognition, through the heightened consciousness previously described, of the reality of the "spiritual world" and of beings of higher intelligence who inhabit it. To their wisdom and guidance human beings owe our present development and capacities.

In those early times, it was the priest or priest-king who guided the individual through his or her attainment of a higher consciousness. We see that this is a recognized factor even in late examples of representations of the Pharaohs, where the inspiring being or beings are placed as small figurines at different parts of the Pharaoh's anatomy—behind the head, or at the base of the spine, for example. The scribe in these early civilizations received the word of the gods from the mouth of the priest or king. If the scribe made an error in impressing the holy word of light into substance (i.e., into darkness), he would be condemned to death. Writing was a highly responsible activity in those times!

This reverence for the holiness of the act of writing was resuscitated in the Christian era by the copying of the Gospels. Monks spent a lifetime writing down the Word of God. The beautiful, pictorial lettering we so much admire was formed out of the content of their meditational activity. The colors they used and the way the incidents were portrayed in the tiny Gospel pictures showed their understanding, gained from their meditation, of these events. They constitute a secret language in itself for the guidance of the reader and the next transcriber. [7]

Living imaginatively into such contexts, we can gain a clearer understanding of why so much fear and opposition was engendered when printing was first invented. The *Word* was divorced from its living source in the human soul; it could be reproduced and fall into any hands without any preparation of the soul for receiving its contents. Here again, working in subconscious depths, is what can be considered a repetition of the Fall of Man from the original spiritual heights of consciousness. One can imagine both the eagerness for knowledge, and its counterpart of subconscious fear, at work in the souls of the people of this period, even in the designation of printing as the "black art" —a fear that has echoed on.

The Arrival of the Alphabet

In his book on the alphabet,[8] Diringer distinguishes between the writings of civilizations which only developed as far as pictograms and ideographs, of which Egyptian hieroglyphs and Assyrian cuneiform are examples, and of those which have developed a concise number of symbols which could be freely used to express the content of the language. He considers only the latter to be true writing, for example, Hebrew and Greek. Through the alphabet the mind is able to express its thought content in words; it becomes the vehicle of a person's conscious intellectual ability.

From his research, Diringer states that the alphabet was the last major form of writing to appear, and that it had its origin at a single point in history, somewhere in the region of present-day Israel/Palestine/Syria.

Writing prior to pictograms and hieroglyphs he described as "writing in embryo" and considered it to consist of signs for ritual and magic, rather than symbols for communication. He observed that the geometric element, which is present at the beginning of a writing system, does not represent a reduction of representational drawing. The symbols appear to convey "static ideas," such as nouns, but not a discourse, which Diringer rightly claims to be the essential element in writing.

He also shows that rudimentary forms of writing were not all developed prior to systematic scripts. Some pictogram forms emerged long after the appearance of alphabetic writing elsewhere.

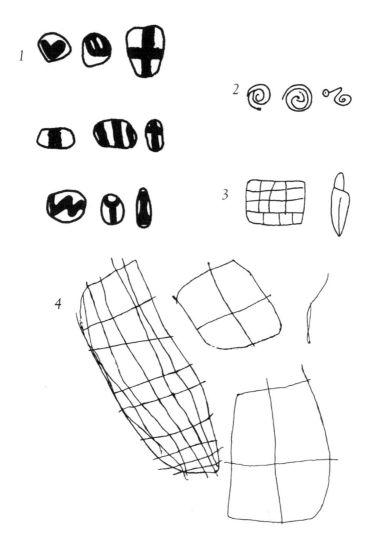

1. Prehistoric conventionalized figures and geometric shapes: printed pebbles of the mesolithic culture, painted with peroxide or iron, from Mas d'Azil, Ariège, South France.

2. Petroglyphs from California.

3. Conventionalized figures and signs from Italy.

4. Windows. Tower full of windows by Héloise, age four years and one month.

A Unique Faculty

If we take the view that writing is closely related to the development of a people from one form of consciousness to another, we can begin to understand why the phenomenon arose.[9] The tribe or nation is recapitulating earlier stages of consciousness before achieving the general intellectual faculty which is the ultimate fruit of the long development of Western civilization. "Writing has been the main currency of civilization. . . . It is the main aspect of culture which clearly distinguishes mankind from the animal world."[10]

Susan Greenfield corroborates this.[11] She tells us that the fine motor movements of our fingers are controlled by a motor pathway exclusive to primates. Dexterity with our hand distinguishes us from all other animals.

These important findings of both earlier and recent research of the twentieth century lead directly to the observation that human beings inwardly bear a creative power which cannot emanate from purely animal faculties, namely that the human being is a *spiritual* being. The immortal soul and spirit being live in the sense-perceptible vehicle of the physical body which is endowed with the powers of life and growth. Humans once knew this in their deepest natures. The intellectual faculty, which during its development closed the door to spiritual perceptions, gave the human race mastery of the earth, though it extinguished the individual's personal knowledge of his own origin.

At the height of this intellectual development, however, there were still people who, through the very power of their thinking, penetrated to concepts of the human being's spiritual origin and the reason for being on earth.

Gotthold E. Lessing (1729–81), writing in the middle of the eighteenth century, was one of these. He reviewed the history of humankind and said that this was not to be seen merely as a fortuitous series of events, but rather that these events were there to develop and educate the human being. Lessing suggested that ". . .each individual needed a lifetime in each of the successive cultural civilizations in order to grow in stature and fulfill his soul and spiritual potential."[12] Later in the nineteenth century, Rudolf Steiner took this concept further. He posited that each human being was his own entelechy whose spirit member, the "I" or "ego," reproduces itself from one earth life to the next, thus undergoing self-development and transformation, which would represent a christian-ized concept of reincarnation.[13]

Implications for Classroom Teaching Today

If we test such concepts and apply them to our work in a practical and imaginative way, we find that they can indeed broaden our outlook and provide new possibilities both for understanding problems and for identi-fying novel solutions for them.

Looking from this perspective, let us imagine a classroom of children. Deep in each child's soul-spirit could be the residue of attitudes and feel-ings from experiences of earlier civilizations and cultures.[14]

Some children may never have confronted the printed word or ever learned to write in such past lives. In others a dim feeling may arise, a memory-association of the awe surrounding the activity of writing in ear-lier times. Others may have a malaise of fears ensuing from some direct experience connected with the first appearance of the printed page. These could be "overtones" within the process of learning that can affect the children's ability to absorb the contents of the lesson.

None of this will come into consciousness; it will be working within the interplay of feelings with movement and the metabolism of the child's will forces. In the same way a child previously exposed to trau-matic events has, when she experiences a potentially threatening situa-tion, unconscious, automatic trauma-related flashback responses. These responses are in the form of emotional, motor (e.g., muscle tension) and/or physical state (e.g., heart-rate, breathing) "memories."[15]

Teachers who are willing to consider such an idea will find that their range of observation increases and that they begin to develop quite another attitude to children's mistakes and clumsiness. In the awkward way a boy or girl handles the pencil, there may be working the memory residue of how a stylus or brush was used. If we recognize such possibili-ties, we are more likely to use a different tone of voice when we again come to show the child how to hold the pencil. Our students will respond to this new inner attitude of ours from their deepest soul nature; the feeling of being understood creates a health-giving bond between child and teacher; forces of life are stimulated; confidence in the authority of the grown-up is strengthened in the right way. A willingness to learn from such a person arises in the student.

To be a true educator each one of us will have to find methods which will free our students from the past, giving nourishment for the seeds of their earlier experiences to come to fruition in a positive way.

CHAPTER 3

THE PREPARATION FOR WRITING

The less we train the intellect directly and the more we aim to train the whole human being in such a way that the intellect will evolve out of the movement of the limbs, out of dexterity, the better it is. [1]

—Rudolf Steiner

The Preschool and Kindergarten Years

We have described how, by the time the young child is able to stand and take her first steps, the threefold elements of space perception— left/right, above/below, and forward/backward—are embedded by movement activity into the physical body. The life forces with which we are endowed, and which have to last us a lifetime, stream down from the head into the body during the first seven years of life. This is why the preschool child lives in quite a different consciousness from that of the adult, different even from the consciousness of a ten-year-old.

During this time the head is really the *center of growth*, and this function should not be disturbed if the human being is to maintain health and vitality throughout life. The *consciousness* of the young child while awake fills her body and limb system. She explores her environment with her limbs and senses. She absorbs everything at this stage of her life in spontaneous and complete empathy with her surroundings, both physical and moral. All her experiences—from the butterfly flitting from flower to flower or the central heating starting up beside her to the effects of her mother's and father's attitudes to life's problems—sink deeply into her. Ask a three- or four-year-old standing in front of a flower bed what the flowers are. She is likely to say, "flower." Tell her, "This flower is a daffodil," then ask her what it is. She will probably still say flower. She lives in a world of universals: all trees are trees; all flowers are flowers. In children who have escaped the process of early intellectualization, differentiation comes much later. This natural state of empathy, which gives her the ability to imitate everything we do and say, is a remnant of the kind of consciousness which she had not so long ago before birth.

Hence the child does not discriminate between what is harmful, beneficial, good, or bad. It is we adults who drive her out of the paradise which has been her sole experience of life and to which she is entirely devoted. We force her out too soon, through our requirement for greater definition and our authoritative attitudes, our wide variety of negations, such as, "Don't ___ !" "Stop it!" "You shouldn't do that."

The alternative does not mean that we allow the child to do as she likes and so become a nuisance to herself and to us. It does, however, create a challenge to our ingenuity, presence of mind, and our will to overcome inner inertia or emptiness within ourselves, so that we train the behavior of the child through her ability to copy us. By our own behavior we set the pattern for what should be done.

Similarly, we have to develop, in ourselves, the knack of diverting the child's attention away from what is harmful or should not be done. Which is easier: to take out of a child's hand something that she should not have, with the resulting scream of rage and tears, or to divert her attention first, for example, by removing one's shoe, if nothing else is available, and making it hop along the table, and gently removing the object from her grasp while her attention is caught by this new impression? If the child still persists in wanting what has disappeared one just says, "All gone," in a tone of voice which contains that meaning.

This faculty for natural positive authority has become rather weak nowadays. Parents tend to resort to shouting at the child, which initiates, of course, a like response from the child, adding to the angry frustration of both. Fortunately, parenting courses are available to help parents to understand this kind of problem. This is the right moment for asserting authority consistent with the child's consciousness because, in the spiritual world in which she has been living, things are beings and thoughts appear and disappear from consciousness. Therefore, "out of sight, out of mind," is a factor which can be assimilated by the child; it is one which is reproducing and recapitulating a state of soul that was part of her pre-earthly experience. Developing this presence of mind and fantasy will, in fact, resuscitate our own life forces and increase our own vitality. Such is the challenge and opportunity our family brings us.

When the change of teeth is in process, this is the sign that the "inner house building," which we have been able to watch through the child's drawings, is being completed. A new form of consciousness is going to arise with a new relationship to her environment and to adults. In short, the child is ripe for school, and the life forces, released from their body building activity, may now be used for formal learning and memory.

Entry into Formal School

The child participating in the Waldorf curriculum enters formal school in the autumn semester which follows the Easter of his sixth year, at the age of six and a half or seven years. He is at an important stage of growing up; his body is now ready for school. And he knows it, too. "I go to school now," he tells us. The kindergarten is now left behind.

In the United Kingdom, the age at which formal school is commenced is around five years, although this is unusually early compared with much of Europe and other parts of the world. The consequence of this for the Waldorf parent is that some peer group pressure, or pressure from friends and family, may be experienced for the period during which the child appears to be behind his contemporaries at schools elsewhere. Ultimately, the test of the approach needs to be assessed in the capabilities of Waldorf students who have completed the fundamental writing and reading skills by the age of eight to nine years. At this stage, there can generally be seen an enthusiasm and mastery which indicate that the student has clearly benefitted, and in no way suffered, from this seeming delay.

A similar issue arises over the timing of the application of the Waldorf approach to handwriting. The Waldorf curriculum determines both the most appropriate developmental age for handwriting and the order in which the elements of handwriting are taught. The Waldorf teacher will follow both these aspects which are felt to be totally interrelated. However, in schools where the age for the teaching of handwriting has been determined to be earlier than in the Waldorf school, the child will still benefit from the sequence in which it is undertaken in the Waldorf approach.

Picture Consciousness

The knowledge we now have to bring to the school-aged child should suit her new stage of consciousness. It should not over-stimulate the nervous system by demanding the understanding of concepts and ideas—even in a play situation—for this will stifle the imaginative faculty, lead to fixed thinking patterns, and burden the memory. It is this that disturbs the organic functions, making some children grow thin and pale, others unconcentrated and disruptive. Children with strong life forces do manage to carry the burden of an intellectual method of teaching, but the unhealthy consequences are likely to appear later in life. Then, the robbing of the life-forces through premature intellectual activity can result in lack of vitality in the bodily processes. The final outcome can be seen in the hardening processes so well known in the medical profession as scleroses of various kinds.[2]

The Waldorf teaching method requires us instead to call on the imaginative picture-consciousness which is awakening in the child. She is now capable of relating herself more consciously to what affects her soul life and to what she experiences from outside. We strive to find a balance in the content of the lessons between what she wants to express and the objective element in the subject itself. For example, she begins to learn that colors have laws and relationships among themselves, and that, if she is to create something beautiful, she cannot just fill in her paper with the colors she likes. Naturally the teacher guides the organic type of self-expression of the kindergarten stage very gently and slowly over into the realm of color harmony and relationships.

Preparing the Child for Writing

Absorbing the Elements of the Letter Forms

Writing, which calls strongly on the nervous system and on a consciousness which is awake and not dreaming, has to be carefully prepared. So, let us look first at the structure of the alphabetic symbols themselves. Self-evidently, the symbols are based solely on the straight line and the curved line. There are, of course, many implications behind this, especially with regard to the orientation in space and the directions of these lines.

We have already described how the body is oriented to space. Let us now observe the pattern of what is straight and what is curved in relationship to nature and to human beings. We experience the curve as soon as we are out of doors. From the horizon before and behind to the zenith there is the blue curve of the sky. We have this curve reflected in the sun's circle and its passage across the heavens. The moon repeats it, adding its exquisite celestial curve when it is new to the straight line of its first quarter. The plant sends up its shoots vertically in response to the influence of these heavenly bodies and assumes an endless variety of forms between vertical and curve during its growth.

In observing the animal, we see how the straight line and the curve are dominated by the horizontal element. The animal's spine is parallel with the earth. It follows the line of the horizon. The structure of the human being has combined all these elements—the horizontal, the vertical, and the curved line—and, from their harmonious relationships, the child experiences a sense of freedom in his soul.

By first grade, this freedom should be objectified in his movements and in his conscious relationship to these forms. The child has been and still is living unconsciously in all these movements of nature. They have been the stimulus, via his senses, for his growth. What we now have to do is to bring the subconscious knowledge of this world pattern into a more conscious relationship with his own organism, through his inner imaginative feeling and activity.

With all of this in mind, the teacher calls on the child to *walk a straight line*, then to *run the line*. Next the teacher asks him to *draw this line in the air*, and to *draw this with his foot*. What difference does he feel? Now the teacher asks him to *draw this line on the blackboard*, and *now on the floor*. We must also ask him where the straight line is in him—in his arm? In his back? We can take eurythmy rods or walking sticks and hold them against our backs and walk forward and backwards. Shall we try to run? Oh, dear! Something else wants to happen: our backs want to bend!

Next we come to the curve. We lie on the floor in curves, we can lie in a straight line, too. Afterwards we can run these forms. We can curve different parts of our body. Someone may discover that our head has a curve in it. Our arms can curve, too, but our legs can only make straight line "curves"—zigzags! We are now well on the way to turning ourselves into patterns.

Straight Lines and Curves

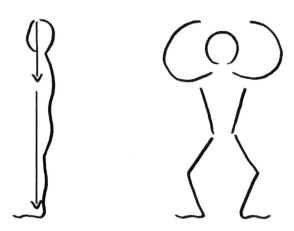

In this way—with other imaginative additions from the individual teacher—the class gains a thorough inner consciousness of the straight line and the curve, the essential elements of handwriting. Through such an experiential approach, we have brought the learning process into an objective feeling relationship with what the child has accomplished during the first years of life through her sensory and movement experiences.

At last the moment has arrived when the children are ready to draw these forms on the paper in front of them. Their brand new beeswax stick crayons are in front of them. But what is this? The crayons themselves are straight, and they have a curve, too! In their very form is embodied the basic pattern for the use to which they will be put. So now all must hold them properly and sit in the right pattern, too.

Practical Preparations: Tables, Chairs, and Posture

We are now at the point when we must consider practical matters, for example, the height of the table or desk in relation to the seat and the size of the child. This is of vital importance if we are to have good writing. Fortunately, modern school furniture designers offer us the means to carry this out. But do we pay enough attention to such factors?

The desk height should not push the arm upward so that one shoulder is higher than the other or so that neither shoulder can relax. The chair can be about ten inches lower than the table height; this depends upon the length of each child's trunk. The child should sit so that both feet are firmly on the floor with the knees higher than the hip joints. This angle between the thighs and pelvis is vital. The child who sits this way, fully into his hip joints, allows the movement of the hand and arm to flow from the base of the spine. This cannot take place if the hip joints are slightly higher than the knees; there is then a pulling on the thigh muscles, creating tension which is experienced through the body all the way to the arm and hand.

The child's movement system responds to such an unequal balance by either turning the feet inwards or curling them around the chair legs, thus producing muscular distortions which curb the whole movement response to eye-hand coordination. The foundation is thus laid for tight pencil gripping, sitting with the weight on one side of the body, or twisting half around at the waist. As a teacher, you do not have to look very far before you see such sitting patterns and their effects on the handwriting!

To encourage good posture, the correct sitting position needs to be presented imaginatively as a picture to the children. For example, the children can sit like a king preparing to sign a royal decree, his feet placed on a footstool, his red robe keeping his right arm to the side of his body, the left hand weighted by a heavy flashing ring of jewels so that all see him move the paper as his right hand writes. And he must hold his head up straight so that his "crown does not fall off!" This picture can be acted out in turn by the children in full royal regalia, and it would be helpful if they all wore crowns loosely placed on top of their heads while writing until good posture habits are firmly established.

«This »

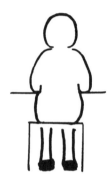

« Not this »

Such a picture needs to be reinforced by the teacher who must be very conscious when he sits down beside a child to write. It enhances his authority if he treats himself as an object and says aloud, "Let me see: Have I put my feet in the right place. Is my arm comfortable?" and so on. Time spent each morning looking to see that each child is properly seated, until the right posture has become habit, is teaching time very well invested.

It has been interesting to discover that, within a year's age range, it is usually only necessary to provide a class with two different heights of tables and chairs. The discrepancy between the varied heights of children is leveled out by the fact that some children have long bodies and short limbs and others have short bodies and long limbs. Footstools can make up the difference when the knees end up lower than the hip joints.

It is of vital importance to draw parents' attention to this matter. The ordinary chair height is seventeen inches, which is usually suitable for those of us who five feet six inches and taller. Table heights correspond to this. Ideally the child only draws and writes at a table suitable for his own height. If this is not possible, use a cushion and a footstool to bring chair and table height into correct relationship. Parents make sure that this is done and gently but firmly insist that the child use what they provide for him. Children unfortunately soon become used to writing while sitting even in awkward positions, even though such positions impair their ease of writing.

Please also advise parents to see that children still have plenty of opportunities to draw their own pictures and to scribble to their heart's content. If we want to develop and keep good handwriting and prevent muscular tension and fatigue, care for these factors must be applied throughout the class teaching time. Scribbling and drawing continue as healthy occupations for the senses, and parents can generally divert more of the child's time in this direction and away from over-stimulating TV and video watching, or playing electronic or computer games.

Letter Forms and Spatial Orientation—
The Teacher's Preparatory Work

Then the moment arrives for the teacher to place visually before the children the two forms which they have run and walked and explored in their bodies: the straight line and the curve. How are these to be placed on a blackboard in relation to the surface as a two-dimensional plane and in relation to each other?

The possibilities include:

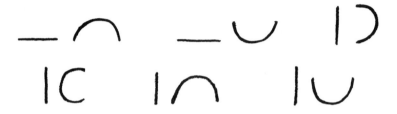

One could reply, "Does it matter? Just draw them as it comes naturally." If one follows this line of reasoning, then one is simply passing on to the child what is instinctive in oneself, instead of trying to penetrate into the language of form and movements. In his art of education, Rudolf Steiner introduced a new subject, that of form drawing, a pedagogical means of developing imagination, inner picturing, and flexible thinking. The indications which he gave have been beautifully worked out and presented in a book by Margaret Frohlich and Hans Niederhäuser entitled *Form Drawing* and more recently in several books by Rudolf Kutzli, as well as one by Ernst Schuberth and Laura Embry-Stine.[3]

Handwriting, as we have said, is concerned with the straight line and the curve, the basic elements of each alphabetic symbol. We are therefore going to look at the straight line and the curve with regard, first, to their directions in space and, secondly, to their relationship with the soul forces of thinking, feeling, and the will. In learning to write, we are reminding the soul of what it has accomplished physiologically in the body during the first seven years of life, as well as leading it on into future stages of developing consciousness. The process of learning to write will link up with the child's experience throughout his school life under the Waldorf curriculum. Besides form drawing, this experience will include gymnastics, geometric drawing in fifth and sixth grade, perspective drawing in seventh grade, and physics from the class teaching period to the high school; it culminates with the nautical mathematics of eleventh grade and the main lesson on architecture in twelfth grade.

Spatial Dimensions

As adults we can be aware when we put our body into a horizontal position, when we lean over diagonally, or stretch to our full height. Rudolf Steiner connects these bodily movements both to space and to our soul powers.

In lectures entitled *Man: Hieroglyph of the Universe*, he asks us to overcome the abstraction of considering the directions of space as purely interchangeable radiating lines. He describes them to us as planes of activity which relate our own soul forces to those working in the universe. He makes us vividly aware of the dynamic difference between the symmetry (sagittal) and vertical (frontal) planes, with the horizontal plane as the mediator. This horizontal plane divides space into above and below; it is connected with the soul force of feeling. The perpendicular (sagittal) plane divides space into left and right; it is the plane of symmetry—the plane of thinking. The vertical (fontal) plane is that which divides the human being into front and back; it is the plane of will. Will in the human being is connected with the movements of going before and behind. Steiner characterizes this by pointing out that our food moves from in front to behind. This plane represents the will activity of our metabolism; the experience of the frontal plane also comes about through our being able to keep ourselves integrated into the rotational movement of the earth. So when we fall over, we have temporarily lost the power of keeping pace with the gyration of the earth!

To bring these planes from the three dimensions of space into the two dimensions of drawing and writing, we need to clarify the difference between the perpendicular (symmetry/sagittal) plane and the vertical (frontal) plane. In the dictionary—and therefore, no doubt, in our own minds—vertical and perpendicular tend to be described as synonymous terms. We must remember, though, that we are speaking of planes of activity, not just lines. The perpendicular—symmetry or sagittal—plane is connected to the right angle. We stand perpendicular to the surface of the earth. Therefore the straight line which we draw from above to below is our symmetry line which divides the paper into left and right, the line of the perpendicular, thinking plane.

The vertical—frontal—plane is the one that divides in the human being what is in front from what is behind. This in two-dimensional space is represented by the lines of perspective which connect one's eye level with a specific point on the horizon. Therefore, when we draw a diagonal line from upper right to lower left, we are drawing the line of the vertical/frontal plane, the line which represents will activity. Physiologically, we can move our eyes up and down (perpendicularly in the symmetry plane), and we can move them to the left and right (in the horizontal plane), but to move the eyes forward and back we have to use our will in order to move our whole body forward and backward. This forward and back movement as expressed in the two dimensions of space on our paper is the diagonal line which connects our eye with the point on the horizon, as in perspective drawing.

Soul Faculties and the Directions of Space

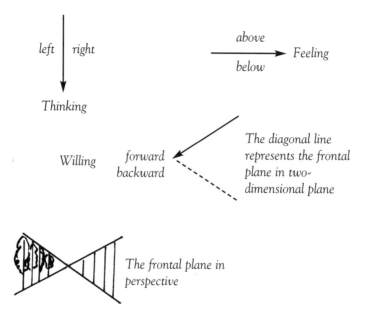

The curve is the sum total of all three planes. It is the boundary between the human being and the universe of the stars. Its qualitative language is that of clockwise and counterclockwise movement. The natural movement of the right arm is clockwise; it moves from left to right. A consecutive clockwise spiral swings from above left to above right, then down—the modern European direction of writing. The left side mirrors this in reverse moving from upper right to upper left, then down.

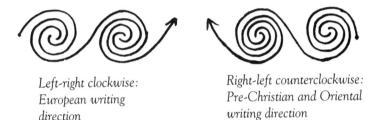

Left-right clockwise:
European writing
direction

Right-left counterclockwise:
Pre-Christian and Oriental
writing direction

In other lectures, Rudolf Steiner discusses the capacities of soul which are built up by the different directions of writing used by the various cultures.[4]

We have now several choices. Do we wish to emphasize the qualitative element of *feeling* by drawing our straight line on the horizontal plane and reiterate this with the clockwise above-below movement of the curve beside it? Or do we wish to emphasize the perpendicular element of *thinking* with its left-right symmetry and bring our curved line in relation to this, then deciding between the clockwise and counter-clockwise direction for the curved line?

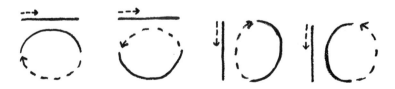

This is for the teacher to ponder and decide in relationship to the particular disposition of the children before him. Is there a preponderance of any one temperament in the class, for example? Is it a dreamy or an awake group of children?

Johannes Kepler (1571–1630) retained throughout his life the religious devotion to the universe that is the special gift of the young child. In him this acted as a heightened consciousness, and from this he was able to give us the three laws of planetary motion. He writes in his work *Harmonicus Mundi*, "In the beginning God on an indisputable decision chose the straight and the curved with which to imprint upon the World the divinity of the Creator."[5]

Rudolf Steiner emphasizes the importance of the impression that is made on the child of his first lesson, where we make him aware of these two fundamental forms—hence the necessity of our conscious preparation. Margaret Frohlich sums this up in the book *Form Drawing* as the teacher's constant awareness of the three guiding questions, and his endeavor to live up to what they imply: What am I to do? How am I to do it? Why am I to do it?[6] This inner attitude will enable the teacher to help the children entrusted to him. This is the standard for the preparation of our lesson, because good honest teaching must be based on the inner attitude of the teacher.

Well, we have left our imaginary classroom some pages back, with its students waiting quietly, we hope, for us to give them something to do. So let us return.

Techniques for Teaching the Line and the Curve

We place our choice of a straight line and a curved line on the blackboard and ask our students to draw these in the air, one after the other. We emphasize that each one is to watch his or her finger as it draws the form, never letting it out of sight. We ourselves notice which children make large free movements with the whole arm and which children do not stretch their arms or only make restricted movements from the wrist.

To avoid cramped handwriting later, we immediately help those children with restricted movement. These children can come up to the blackboard to each trace the teacher's large drawings on the board with one finger, thus generating movement which uses the whole muscular system of the arm.

Meanwhile, the teacher can use this opportunity to develop the skill of maintaining the interest of the children who did not have restricted movement and who are sitting at their desks during this process. The cultivation of an interest in each other is an important part of social moral training.

When we are satisfied that the children with cramped movements have experienced a release from their restrictions, the forms can be erased and replaced by those children who have good, free arm movement. They, too, may each draw the forms in a very large size, using the whole arm, not just the wrist.

The next step is to ask each child to cover or close one eye and trace the forms in the air with one hand, using the open eye to closely watch the tracing hand. This process will show the teacher the prevailing eye and hand dominance in each child as each one chooses eye and hand this *first time*. Dominance will be discussed in a later chapter.

Repeat this tracing of the forms in the air with one hand, now with both eyes closed. Finally, trace this imaginary form with movements of the eyes, while the eyes actually remain closed. It is important that the teacher makes sure the children move their eyeballs by using imaginations, for example, by having them pretend that their eyes can magically see through the closed eyelids how the hand traces the forms.

So that good eye-hand coordination and attentive looking will become habitual, this procedure is repeated with every new pattern which they are to draw in their books or on their form drawing paper. After noticing and recording discrepancies between students' choices of sides for eye and hand the first time this was done, it is important to teach them to keep open *the eye on the same side* as the writing hand. Thus, if the right hand is the writing hand, the child closes the left eye—preferably muscularly, but if necessary, by using the left hand to cover the left eye—or vice versa.

A further possibility is to tell every other child to draw the given form on the neighbor's back. The neighbor then repeats the form in the air in front of him before turning around to draw it on the first one's back.

With this method we can draw all sorts of patterns based on the straight line, curve, and loop during the first two school years. Implicit in such forms are the shapes of the capital letters and the clockwise and counter-clockwise movement of the arch and cup letters of the cursive alphabet, which will be taught during second grade.

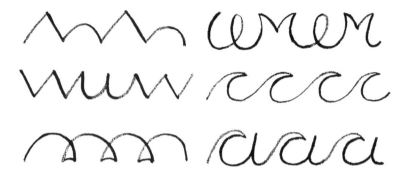

The Cultivation of Motor Skills

The drawing of patterns is done very carefully on large sheets of paper. The children practice drawing the straight lines in different spatial directions. Make sure the strokes use the full width of the page. First horizontal lines are drawn left to right across the form drawing page, next a page of vertical lines drawn from above down. Then the spatial directions may be drawn in blocks of lines at least 12" (30cm) in length, three different ways—one page each time; see below.

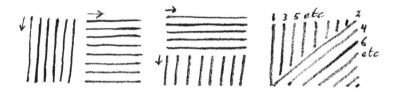

Experienced teachers are observing more and more children with poor motor skills. Fingers and wrists are no longer as dexterous as they were ten or twenty years ago. Our present culture and environment have deprived the children of practicing many of the skills which belong to the previous stage of development (see chapter 7). We need to give them the opportunity to recapitulate these stages.

For example, stirring an enormous, heavy Christmas pudding dough (as this needs effort, a right-handed child will circle counter-clockwise from outside inward, maybe even using both hands) or winding a giant ball of wool (circling from the center up and outwards) are activities which could reactivate the scribbling whirl of the young child's first drawings.[7] When beating an egg, which does not need much effort, a right-handed person generally beats clockwise, just as when winding the ball of wool. Drawing to-and-fro pendulum rhythms from one side of the paper to the other could follow the experience of the children when, sitting opposite each other on the floor, they join hands and swing to-and-fro as they sing a rowing song.

During the first years of grade school, this kind of free movement drawing can gradually be formalized into running cursive patterns across the page. Careful observation will show when the children are ready for this. The wool, wound into its ball, can now be "pulled out" into a looping pattern across the page. Straight lines can cross and become a rhythmic pattern: zigzags, spirals. There are many imaginative variations for making such patterns.

With a two- or three-week block of an introductory main lesson of such movement and form drawing activities as these and with those previously described, we should be ready to introduce the capital alphabetic letters to the children. A child begins with movements, expressions of will, not with looking at things. That comes later. Hence it is necessary to begin, not with reading, but with writing—but a writing which comes naturally from the whole human being.[8]

Practical Applications and Summary

- Teachers, please check desk height, pencil hold, and writing techniques.

- The height of desks and chairs: the ideal is that each desk and table height allows the forearm of the writing hand to be supported to about two inches from the elbow without having this shoulder drawn up or down. This is vital as a lack of proper support causes muscle tension in the hand, arm, and shoulder.

- Children's postures when they draw the running forms and when they write: when the child is sitting at the desk, make sure that both feet are placed firmly on the floor with the right foot slightly in front of the left (for right-handers). Crouching over the desk or holding the head to one side is not allowed; shallow breathing, poor circulation, indigestion, and fatigue can be the consequences.

- The paper or exercise book is placed parallel to the front of the desk and a little to the right of center. This position for the right-handed person is that of the professional calligrapher, for the artist always has an innate feeling for the correct relationship of his materials and tools to that of his body. Originally desks were sloped so the students did not have to bend their heads forward, which causes a neck strain.

- For right-handers, the function of the left hand is to pull the paper upwards towards the top edge of the desk, drawing it as necessary toward the left, so that the right hand and arm are not forced into a turned out position with the hand too far off to the right. The writing hand should not be allowed to slide downward to the edge of the desk and so lose support for the forearm.

- Make sure crayons and pencils are not less than 4.5 inches (10.5 cm) long when new. As soon as they no longer rest against the base of the first finger, or the side of the hand between thumb and first finger, an extension can be made and attached, or the pencil or crayon should be discarded for writing purposes.

- Make sure the crayon, and later the pencil, is correctly held from the first time the student picks it up off the desk in front of him. The physiologically correct grasp has the end of the long finger supporting the pencil or crayon with the tips of the first finger and thumb resting next to each other above the pencil. (See drawing on book cover.) This grasp allows the hand to rest on its side and the forearm to be in neutral position between pronation and supination; thus, both gross and fine motor movements are in balance. A tight grip inhibits fine movement control, leading to tension in the muscles of the upper arm and those of the neck, leading to quick fatigue. An incorrect grasp on the pencil will also affect the fluency and speed of writing so necessary for dictation and note taking in later classes. Therefore immediate attention to this important detail is a teaching must. (For reasons why children avoid using this grasp, see chapter 7.)

- Before drawing the forms the children can:

  1. Run and walk them;

  2. Find them in their bodies;

  3. Draw them in the air with the writing hand, eyes carefully following the motions of the moving finger as previously described. (When the teacher first gets to know a child, a free choice of hand and eye and foot can be given so that the teacher can observe the child's handedness as well as eye and foot preference.)

- The forms can be drawn in the air in the following sequence (for right-handed students):

  1. Right hand with both eyes open, closely following the moving hand and/or finger;

  2. Right hand with only right eye open, carefully following the tracing hand/finger;

  3. Right hand with both eyes closed, yet moving along as if they could see the moving finger;

  4. The eyes move the form while closed; the teacher can observe each student's moving eyeballs under the closed eyelids.

- Variations:

  1. Every other child draws a form on the back of the child who sits next to him; this child then draws the form in the air, on his paper, or on the blackboard.

  2. Draw forms on paper on the floor with the right foot (for right-handers), the pencil held between the big and second toes. Left-handed children use left eye, left foot. (For their writing postures, see chapter 7, pages 104–106.)

Children's Eyes

Teachers, please advise parents to have their children's eyes tested as early as three years of age to make sure their child is perceiving clearly. The first five years are critical in the establishment of normal vision. I am informed by an ophthalmologist that by the time a child enters school, "lazy eye" (ambliopia) can be dense and useful vision irretrievable. Eye strain must be avoided. Teachers must see that the eyes are held the distance from the paper as is the length from the elbow to the knuckle of the first finger. For an adult this is 12–14 inches (37–38 cm.). One eye should not be held nearer the paper than the other.

CHAPTER 4

TEACHING THE LETTERS
AS PICTURES

The qualities of childhood pass over into later life through a metamorphosis determined by quite definite laws.[1]

There is always an urge in the soul to pass from a unity to its parts.[2]
—Rudolf Steiner

These two educational concepts lie at the heart of Steiner's pedagogy. He emphasizes again and again that they require from the teacher an artistic feeling and approach to his subject. Education is an art, and the teacher must become an artist both in the presentation of his subject and in the handling of his students. This idea is reiterated in lecture after lecture. If we teachers fully accept this as reality, our students will be able to develop, or at any rate will have better chances to develop, an intellectual capacity with a healthy constitution. They will develop a sixth sense of how to act in our rapidly changing social conditions and the courage and confidence to deal with those problems which life will present them.

Writing and reading are two highly complex activities which are today required of our children at an extremely early age. "Now it is a thoroughly unnatural thing to require a child in its sixth or seventh year to copy, without more ado, the signs which in this advanced stage of civilization we now use for writing," Steiner said to teachers at Oxford in 1922.[3]

How then are we to meet the demands of our present educational requirements without taking from our children the life-forces they need for their organic development, for natural and healthy digestion systems, for their breathing, the functioning of their hearts, the co-ordination of their limbs, the proper physical growth of the brain itself?

This question stands behind all of Steiner's art of teaching. He points out that the demand for precocious intellectual activity, which we see as a general educational trend today, may cause the physical organs and the whole nervous system of the child to become likely preys for all sorts of malfunctioning. His soul easily grows apathetic to his environment, often even strongly antipathetic to his lessons and even to his whole education. We all know how nowadays truancy from school has become widespread and is of great concern to the educational authorities.

The Principle of Recapitulation

To counter these sad happenings and to forestall the infinite number of support/remedial lessons that are having to be given to help present-day normal students, Steiner suggests that we follow the course of historical development (as described in chapter 2), that we initially present the letters of the alphabet as pictures.

Those of our ancestors who were guardians, or recorders, of the religious secrets of the community were also superb picture makers, to which the cave paintings of Lascaux in the Dordogne bear witness.[4] Only by slow degrees over millennia did human beings acquire the skills which enabled them to reproduce, out of artistic imitation, the material world they saw around them in the pictures which later became symbols for a writing system such as hieroglyphs, cuneiform, and at long last, the formalized characters of Greek, Latin, Hebrew, and Arabic.

Before a baby is born, she is an embryo—a work of art, with the artist, as it were, working on herself. (The ego is taking part from the spiritual world, entering into the organism at the moment of birth.)[5] She does this by recapitulating, during the nine months in her mother's womb, all the complex stages of human development. She is laying into herself the very elements of her humanity, and after her birth she goes on doing it in that larger womb of the home which her father and mother provide for her. She is not a miniature adult. She does not spring like Athena, fully armed, from her father's forehead.

No, she is life's do-it-yourself production, an embryonic human being who must be allowed to go on for about seven years following her own painstaking artistic development in relationship to mature human beings. We cut off this process at her peril; on us depends whether she becomes a hypochondriac in the second half of her life. So let her go on for a little longer following the basic principles of nature, proceeding from the whole to the part. When she later comes into the classroom and can make straight lines and curves with full zest, having had a chance to learn this out of the dynamic of her whole body, then we may write a word for her on the blackboard and tell her what it says.

Most of the letters of the English alphabet, both capital and lower case forms, are made by young children as art gestalts.[6]

Introducing the Consonants

Children today are soon familiar with letters; they see them printed on the cereal packets at breakfast, dancing around on the TV screen, and glaring down from the billboards as the car flashes past them on the way to school. How can these letters, foreign bodies, be brought into relationship with the children's own experience of the natural world of human beings and of nature which they lived so strongly in empathy with in their early years? Need they be thrust from the Garden of Eden into an intellectual desert all at once?

It is interesting to see that, in his sample lesson to the first Waldorf school teachers, Rudolf Steiner chose the word *bath*, for, as he says, it is good to bring the children's attention to this necessity. (Speaking thus in 1919, he gives one a glimpse of the social conditions at the time.) What should be the word for today, in this noisy couldn't-care-less atmosphere which children are absorbing? The children should copy the chosen word, drawing the letters just as they would the forms which they have mastered in the earlier form drawing lessons (in a Waldorf school, the previous block of main lessons). The children say the word clearly until they become aware of the initial sound. Then the letter representing this sound is transformed into a picture for them. The teacher's fantasy and artistic ability are now called upon; there can be as many pictures for this letter as there are teachers! The form of the letter, the picture, and sound must be an organic whole, not a mnemonic aid as in B for BAT. Steiner draws a BEAR, in the shape of the letter B, for the letter B.[7]

The next step is naturally to discover other words beginning with the same sound, and the following day to find words where the sound occurs in a different part of the word.[8] He goes even further and gives a whole sentence as the starting point, analyzing it into words and from the word again to the initial letter. This analysis—and he does not mean grammatical analysis but the separation of the parts off from the whole, like spreading out the inside of a watch, which so many children want to do if they get the chance—is an activity which works deeply in the subconscious part of the soul. This element is ignored in most educational methods. Usually only our intellectual faculty of synthesis is used, leaving the deep principle of analysis unused. The consequence of this is that there emerges from the soul life in later years a tendency to remain in the atomistic concepts of the nineteenth century. This materialistic thinking contradicts the wholistic picture of the human being as part and parcel of his whole environment. This tendency today still separates physics from the biological sciences and bedevils their development.

Steiner elaborates this tendency and continues, "It is simply the unsatisfied impulse to analyze which gives such encouragement to materialism. . . . What serves us for the awakening of unconsciousness in the child is the analysis of sentences and words. . . . Along these lines we bring the child to a genuine inwardness. . . . We develop in him an indication to face the world with a wide awake soul."[9]

Through this method of teaching, we are laying the foundations in the child for a feeling of security about what arises in her as an inner life when she achieves adulthood. It will then have for her an authentic reality and objectivity, which will give her an assurance that is sadly lacking among people of the present time.

The examples which Steiner gives in his lectures always have to do with something directly related to a child's experience. For example, he uses the form of the upper lip for the letter M (mouth), for the letter F the shape of the fish which she has seen, or would have seen in those days, in the market as she came to school. The picture is drawn for the child so that its position will relate to the shape of the written letter. We can use our ingenuity in showing how the form of the D stands upright; Steiner takes the German word *Dach* 'roof' and shows how the D has been turned from facing upward as in the roof to facing the right.[10] (It is interesting to note that the Assyrians used a similar process with their

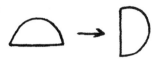

pictograms by turning them 90 degrees to the left; then they proceeded to write from right to left.)

Having established the principle that the form of the letter, its sound, and the picture form an organic whole, the teacher is free to carry the process in any direction she wishes. However, she must be clear in her mind that she is not teaching the letters in order for the child to read and spell, but is introducing the letters, each in its own right, with its intrinsic value, individual form, and sound. Steiner has given a sequence of the consonants which work as forming, creative powers into the life-forces of the human being. If we contemplate the single sounds of the alphabet in this way, we ourselves can come to an idea of how the soul-spirit of the child works on herself as an embryo, each consonant sounding within the mother's organism and working from there as growth/construction powers in the fetus. It was not so long ago that people had a feeling for the deep truth of the statements: "And God said, 'Let there be light,'" and, "In the beginning was the Word."

Such contemplation can alter our attitude. Our attitude is reflected even in the way we write the letters on the blackboard. It is our more thoughtful and conscious attitude which awakens in the children's souls the wish to learn and work. This is, after all, what we are on this earth to do.

The teacher, having jettisoned for the present all her learning on phonetics, can make a story for the picture which she selects for each consonant, or she may weave a story around several of them as, for example, Rudyard Kipling has done in his intriguing story "How the Alphabet Was Made."[11] It is not necessary to transform every letter in this way; as many should be done as are needed to give the children a feeling of having a secure relationship to the use of symbols. These symbols which are presented in their picture form are drawn and painted. Then sentences are made and written on the blackboard by the teacher. The teacher tells (reads) what he has written, and the children then discover the letters they have learnt, finally writing them slowly, with emphasis on the drawing element.

We continue to practice the consonants that have been learnt in this way, writing them in the air, repeating the movements with the eyes closed. We try to discover which children are weak in inner visualization. Then the children run the forms of the letters on the floor, and finally we see that every child can write at least her own name clearly with her right foot (left foot for left-handers), a crayon firmly grasped between her big and first toes, the other foot holding the paper properly on the floor.[12] (Brown paper or the backs of old practice paper can be used for this). We thus bring the child's will fully into play, sending what has been grasped in the head through the whole body by means of a consciously directed movement of will.

This is how the consonants are to be introduced. They are the sounds and signs which have arisen from a copying of the outside world.

Introducing the Vowels

The vowels present us with a different element. No longer is the outside world the inspiration for their picture, but rather the answer which comes from the human being's inner experience of the world around him. The soul responds to the majesty of the sunrise in wonder. Deep from within him wells up the sound *ah*. Before a ravine or hurtling waterfall the mood is one of awe, a mixture of wonder and fear: this sound is *oo*. The *oh* of joy and rapture and the response *(h)ey*, when one feels oneself under attack, are all sounds of the responsive soul to the different experiences it undergoes.

In German these vowel sounds exactly coincide with the written symbols (letters) and with the gesture which is formed in the air by the breath passing through the larynx when they are spoken. Steiner describes how the breath forms itself into a straight line when the English sound of *ee* (the sound represented in German by the letter *i/I*) is made. In other words, in the German language the form of the letter symbol I exactly corresponds with the shape of the breath formed when the name of this letter is spoken. When we write this letter I in English, it looks the same as in the German, but its sound is different, and in English it is the name each person calls himself, "I." In English, the sound *ee* is represented in writing by the symbol E or e whose forms have no relationship to the breath formation of which Steiner speaks; hence complications ensue when transferring his indications to the English language. Many solutions have been attempted, but in view of the increase of dyslexic symptoms in so many English-speaking children nowadays, and the confusion that the writer has observed in older students, the following considerations may be of guidance to teachers facing this problem for the first time.

Ask anyone what the vowels are in English and they will usually answer by giving the names of the symbols: A, E, I, O, U. Here we have an interesting discrepancy of sounds, sounds that express something of the genius of the soul orientation of the language. The vowel sound *ah* as in the word father—in German the letter A—is omitted in this English vowel sequence. In English this same symbol A has to serve both for *ah* and for English *a* as in age, and the symbol I for the English sound *i* actually represents a diphthong *(ah-ee)*. As mentioned, this is also the word in our language that we use to designate our self (ego) in its most inward nature. In the English language the I of our being maintains an objective consciousness of itself within the varied experiences of the soul. For the interested reader, something towards an understanding of this is indicated in Steiner's lectures entitled *The Christ Impulse and the Development of Ego-Consciousness*, but to discuss this here would be out of context. As teachers we have to balance the importance and reverence which Steiner had for the individuality of the different languages with the indication he gave in a specific one (German) as a principle for introducing the symbols of the letters.

By using moods from stories, we must make our students fully aware of the glory of the full tones of the vowel sounds *ah, a, e, i, o, oo*—of their inner contents and the different contexts and soul moods in which these are called forth. But in English the difficulty is in writing these vowel *sounds* as *letters*. As mentioned, we designate vowels as names, not as the soul mood sounds they make. As we discussed, in the German each vowel *name* and *sound* coincides with the soul mood. In English, it can lessen the confusion for the child if the vowels, like the consonants, are taught in a picture form with the words appearing out of a story, but with this difference: the picture must clearly say the *name* of the vowel, in contrast to the pictures for the consonants which have as their basis sound, name, and form of the letter. With the vowels the following is noted: the sound of the first letter in the word ANGEL itself names the vowel; later on the first letter in APPLE can give the short phonetic sound for the same letter. Now draw a picture of an angel so that the shape of the letter A appears in the angel. The picture thus gives the name of the vowel. You can similarly use EAGLE and draw it so the letter E is seen in the soaring eagle's body and wings.

Here again the picture shows the name of the vowel. ELEPHANT can be used for the short vowel sound. Princess IDONIA—when she is *little* (i), she likes to wear her crown every day—can be drawn so that the letter I appears; IMP can be used for the short vowel sound. The word OPAL can be used for O, drawn as an opal ring, for instance; use ORANGE for the short vowel sound. With the word UNICORN the form of the U can appear between the horn and the ears; UMBRELLA is good for the short vowel sound. For the English vowels these are the name/symbol sounds which the child has already heard and been given when she has asked, "What does that letter say?"

Remember that it is the name of the vowel which is used in spelling! "How do you spell father, Mummy?" asks the child. "F, A (as in fate), T, H, E (as in feet), R," comes the reply, his mother saying each letter by its name. This is what the child is confronted with at home; very few parents will split the word up into its sound syllables. "And how do you spell Rita's name?" To the child it sounds like Reetah. "R, I (!), T, A," is the answer. The child needs the security of knowing what to write and will soon learn the names of the letters (sound symbols).

In the first year at school, reading is an imitating activity, given through the authority of the teacher. For example, the teacher points to the word *father* and says, "Father." This is accepted by the child and memorized to the best of his ability. Through writing and meeting the word again and again, it is gradually learned. We can speak of the vowels as the "singing sounds" which make words come alive. The consonants are the "shaping sounds" which envelope the vowels like a cloak. The children can sing the vowel sounds, then place a consonant in front of them. They love to sing, "Bah, bay, be, bi, bo, boo." This can be written down, and the adventurous ones will soon carry this activity further. It is important for teachers in English-speaking Waldorf schools to realize that the sound gestures of the vowels shown and practiced in the eurythmy lessons[13] have, for children in the first grade, simply nothing to do with the written characters.

All the letters and their sounds which the children have learned can be summed up in a sentence which has a moral overtone, for example: THE WORLD IS GOOD. This is an experience of the empathy in which the child has lived in the first seven years of life. Something of this element is called into consciousness when he writes his first sentence. The earlier sentences from which words and letters were analyzed were given by authority and copied through his ability to draw forms. Now the letters are to be written with a feeling/knowing consciousness; the content of the sentence and the choice of words can arise between the teacher and the children. The sentence may first be written with all the letters drawn in their picture form and afterwards repeated, written as plain Roman capital letters, or this second way may be left until the next main lesson. It will depend entirely on the ability of the children and the teacher's sensitivity as to the whole artistic form which the main lesson takes.

Capital Letters: Their Recapitulation of the Spatial Development in the Child

There remains only the decision regarding the style of writing the capital letters. It is of course natural for the teacher to choose the style which he himself uses. Rudolf Steiner intimated that the Roman capitals should come first before the Gothic style of the German calligraphy. At the present time there are many sensory stimuli which interfere with the child's natural abilities. For example, in cartoons the lines constructing houses and geometric figures are formed arbitrarily. All this stimulation interferes with the spatial relationship which the child has developed in his body and with the corresponding relationship to the space around him in home, garden, and street. As this spatial element is disturbed or already lacking in children who have been found to have reading difficulties, it would seem appropriate for the teacher to choose Roman capitals. In them the children will become subjected to the discipline of the upright stroke which helps to make them conscious of left and right. The horizontals of E, F, H, L, T, Z cause them to notice above and below, and the diagonal strokes required for Z, Y, X, W, V, K recapitulate the will element of forward and backward (see Chapters 1 and 3). Writing the capital letters gives children the opportunity to repeat that process by which they are enabled to settle comfortably into their physical bodies. These forms of the capital letters make the body an instrument to reflect the threefold powers of thinking, feeling, and willing. Writing the capital letters works on the child's physical body spiritually through the re-experiencing of three-dimensional space (the three planes of space mentioned in chapter 3 Spatial Dimensions).[14]

Basic form

Letters enclosing space

Letters with partially enclosed space

Curved line open letters

Three-dimensional line open letters

These numerals are often incorrectly written

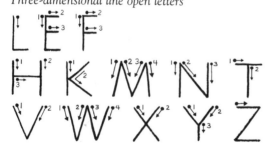

It is important that teachers themselves master the directional movements (above to down, left to right) of each letter, pointing these out as they write the letters on the blackboard. First grade children still have the remains of the imitative faculty of the first seven years. When the teacher's action and speaking are combined, he is more effective than when merely describing, then showing afterwards what has to been done.

All of the above constitutes the first main lesson block in writing. All our efforts in this first school year should be directed to seeing that the children really become at home in this subject and that their work is as perfect as possible; every page of writing should be a picture in itself. This includes proper spacing between the commencement of the sentence and the edge of the paper and space around the writing. Along with this goes the discipline of correct posture, an essential to good work; correct pencil grip, proper muscle control, healthy breathing, and undamaged eyesight are equally important aspects of writing. These aspects are the essentials, not hurrying on in order to attain "proper" reading ages. It will take the first grade teacher all his time and strength to see that the children in his class are sitting and working with good bodily coordination.[15]

The Main Lesson and its Content

All main lessons in a Waldorf school are taught in block lessons, usually of three to four weeks, every morning for the first one and a half to two hours of the day. The work described above would form the intellectual content of the main lesson. Also included in the main lesson will be fairy tales, stories of everyday happenings created by the teacher, class recitation, playing wooden recorders, form drawing, and individual work for particular children or groups—work which is of a pedagogical nature. The activities of the main lesson should call upon the willing, feeling, and thinking elements at work in the soul of each child. The teacher's sensitivity to the children's needs and his artistic feeling for the content of the lesson should engender a sense of well-being in the children, so that body and soul grow together in harmony.

Practical Applications and Summary

. . . you only need a brain when you are moving. For stationary life forms a brain is no longer needed.[16]   —Susan Greenfield

- Drawing and painting the picture of the consonants.

- Running the forms of the consonants.

- Writing consonants in the air using the sequences given in chapter 3.

- Singing the vowel sounds.

- Singing and saying the vowel sounds with a consonant in front of each one.

- Singing and saying the alphabet both forward and backward.

- Accompanying this speech with movement: walking and clapping.

- Clapping above and below alternate legs while walking (or sitting) and speaking.

- Writing their own names, letters, and words with the right foot (left foot for left-handed children).

- Writing the first sentence. The next step is for the children to write their own sentences, in groups and alone.

- For practice time, nursery rhymes and verses from poems that have been learned can be written out by the teacher on large paper in capital letters and pinned on the wall; children can be encouraged to find, out of these "wall verses," a verse they know and copy this in their books. A new verse that will be learned later can also appear on the wall. This will challenge the more awake children, keeping them occupied.

- Teacher concentrates attention on: sitting position, correct holding of the writing instrument, and the eyes. Where are the short-sighted children sitting? No turning of the head sideways so that one eye is strained.

- Train the left hand to do its work: holding the paper, moving the paper up the desk, drawing the paper to the left so that the writing hand does not move too far away from its side of the body.

- Careful drawing of the capital letters. Spacing the letters comes after forming the letters has been properly learned. Some children will maintain the connection with the original pictures of the letters, even as late as class five (ten to eleven years old)—embellishing T as a tree with leaves and apples, giving a K as a king a crown and a scepter; they should not be disturbed in this, nor made conscious of it, nor stopped.

- Children who finish writing quickly should have some handwork which they can do. Finger knitting, braiding/plaiting, colored darning, paper folding, or string games are suitable.

- A booklet of the vowel sounds can be made. A door which opens in the center can show the picture of the vowel.

- Teachers, please look at your own handwriting and notice the way you draw the capital letters. Are the sequences of the strokes correct? Some may be correct for the cursive and italic hands, but are they correct for the Roman capitals that are being taught? See illustrations.

- Teachers: remember that handwriting is character building!

First, we—that is everybody—should recognize our own handwriting as an art—an amazing art really—that should be improved rather than degraded. This is partly for its own sake, and also because it is only from a general interest in, and recognition of, art that any improvement in the forms of the things we produce from pots to cities, can spring up. Common interest in the improvement of ordinary writing would be an immense disciplinary force: we might reform the world if we began with our own handwriting, but we certainly shall not if we do not begin somewhere.[17]

—William Lethaby

Further Notes

- The basic teaching principle is: From the whole to the part.[18]

- Remember the need to satisfy in childhood the analytical tendency working in the subconscious. This means analysis of sentences into words, words into letters.[19]

- Drawing pictures of the letter forms can *first* be done with the paintbrush in a painting/drawing style.[20]

- Once the children have learned to form the letters correctly through speaking the letter names as they write them, they can write their own sentences. They can ask for the spelling of a particular word which the teacher then writes on the board for the child to copy. Avoid too much copying of the text from the blackboard. Eventually compositions as examples from stories can be dictated and punctuated by the teacher so construction and punctuation of sentences is taught. Single words can be written on the board as part of this dictation work. After this children can write their own compositions out of the story material, guided by the teacher.

- There is an example of the first school lesson given by Rudolf Steiner to the first teachers of the Waldorf School.[21]

- Rudolf Steiner also describes the Waldorf approach to writing, reading, and spelling in this same lecture series to the first teachers before the first Waldorf school opened in Stuttgart, Germany, in 1919.[22]

WITHOUT YOUR LIGHT
NO JOY COULD BE
LOOK DOWN GREAT
SUN AND SHINE ON ME

CHAPTER 5

READING YOUR OWN
HANDWRITING

In reading, only the head is occupied and anything that occupies only a part of
the organism and leaves the remaining parts impassive should be taught as late
as possible. The most important thing is first to bring the whole being into
movement, and later on the single parts.[1]

— Rudolf Steiner

This precept we have tried to follow in the classroom work of the children in their first school year. After the presentation of the letters in the first semester, the children will write out selected parts of the fairy tales they have heard. This will be done in the capital letters in large writing books without lines. They read firstly from what is written on the blackboard and then from the writing in their own books.

There is no need for the teacher to use vocabulary suitable to the children's ages and understanding, either orally or in writing the stories. We want them to experience language, their mother tongue, in its beauty, variety, and rhythm.[2] Writing long words of many letters will keep the children's attention occupied and is far better for them than struggling to read the printed page. Descriptive words, beautiful sounding words, will give them the wide range of vocabulary which they will need in later classes. Eight to nine years is the age when children love to "taste" sounds; witness the joy that swear words give them to the mortification of many a mother! So let them exercise this desire in acquiring from their writing a wide variety of exciting sounding and neat looking words. Their very sound and the content of the story will explain their meaning without need for the teacher to give definitions. We have of course to be awake to the ever-changing meaning of the words. Not so long ago a description of the princess descending the stairs, her train sweeping behind her, was met with gasps of astonishment and howls of "Impossible!" The storyteller was visualizing the princess clad in gold and purple velvet, the hearers were seeing the blue and white of the trains of the British Railways! Also, the teacher has to learn how to build up a widening vocabulary for children who are word-starved at home.[3] Limiting the vocabulary is not the answer to this. Waldorf education provides a gift of inestimable value in the eurythmy lessons which awaken a sense for language; eurythmy is a subject which can be taught in any school, state or independent. But the deciding factor is the *telling*—not reading—of stories by parents and teachers. The effort that the adult makes to portray the content of the words by the imaginative situation in which they are used—this is the stimulus which widens the child's interest in sound and words and therewith the intelligence to comprehend their meaning.

Reading Techniques

Reading aloud together, as a class, passages from the blackboard, which the students have already written in their books, helps to establish good intonation and a rhythmic flow of breath. The teacher reads a complete sentence expressively and clearly, and the children repeat it afterwards. Each time the teacher will point to the writing as the children speak. When the children can read the passage as a whole, the teacher turns the children's attention to the individual words, underlining them, finding similar words, those beginning with the same letter, finding out how many times a particular word occurs in a passage, etc. Finally, some of the children may read the passage alone from their books. (Learning to read is not a time-and-motion study).[4]

The following day, after a new piece of writing has been treated in the same way, the previous passage can be read by the student as he walks, taking a step for each word, turning round to go in the opposite direction at a full stop (period). This can be done in various ways, either to suit the temperament of the child, for example, or to help with speech/limb coordination. Teachers will find endless indications in Rudolf Steiner's lectures on how to help children who are asleep in the head, or too nervously awake in their nervous systems, or weak in their breathing and circulatory systems. A teacher should also be observing which children remember easily and which cannot recall what they have learned.[5] Such hindrances can be helped by the methods we use in dealing with the subject matter. The child who has a "sleepy head" will also probably have poor speech/movement coordination, so he should say a word on every step he takes as he reads aloud. Those who cannot recall what they learn should stand and read a sentence, then take three or five steps before reading the next sentence. Others who retain everything in their heads so that they become "gabbling" readers, without any feeling for the structure of a sentence or its meaning, need to read and run (slowly) at the same time.

When children are reading individually, the teacher supports the reading by whispering the word or whole sentence so that there is no hesitation over the unknown word. At the end of the week the children can be asked to write down their favorite words; some can come to the blackboard and write their words for the others to read. The teacher will find endless combinations of this kind of activity and individualizing to meet the capacities the children have. By Easter of the first grade year, if not sooner, the children will have gained a mastery over the size with which they draw/write their letters, the spacing of the words, and awareness of how many words will fit across the page. This being so, it is now time to introduce margins and lines into the children's writing books. The teacher can already have written his passage on lines on the blackboard so that it presents a specially attractive picture. The children are now made conscious of this, and the teacher can draw lines in their books as a guide. There is no need for these to be rigid; a gentle curve allows for more letters. The teacher must explain that the letters walk carefully along the line and must not fall off it at the end, but go at once to a new line. Children soon begin to recognize that a new line is needed when a long word comes near the end of a line.

Introducing Joined—Cursive—Writing

The curriculum of the first school year in Waldorf schools is a recapitulatory summing up of the child's soul-spiritual development during the period up to the change of teeth: his mastery of the muscular system which enables him to move in space, his manual skills, his speech, and social relationships.

The following period of seven years (ages 7–14) is centered physiologically on the growth and development of the breathing and circulatory systems, that rhythmic center in each one of us that sustains our life and never tires! It is the physical expression of the feeling life of the soul. While this is developing, a new stage of consciousness appears in the child. He begins to live in the feeling of the drama of events at home and at school and of his own changing soul life. Sympathy and antipathy as healthy forces of the soul now come to the fore, and the subject matter of our lesson must assure that these forces are fully used, for their fruit will be the faculty of balanced judgment after puberty. This rhythmic element and pronounced feeling will become apparent from the second school year. ("Oh, Mommy, I must have Rosemary to tea today; no not Jane, too; I can't stand her!" These are the signs of the time.) Just as the straight line gave the structure for the child's spatial experience and is basic to the Roman capitals, so the curve is basic to the minuscules. In most lower case letters (minuscules) the rhythmic swing of clockwise and counterclockwise is present.

The Basic Movements of the Minuscles

n   *has an up and over movement — clockwise*

u   *has an up and under movement — counter-clockwise*

The few exceptions embody both these movements.

These two movements are the basic gesture of the right (clockwise) and left (counter-clockwise) arms. These movements sum up all the spatial elements and bring them into a dynamic rhythm. This of itself educates and cultivates a new stage of body-soul development which takes place especially between seven and nine years when the heart and breathing rhythms adjust to that of the adult tempo. A healthy life of body and soul depends on this adjustment's taking place properly.

In the classroom the question which concerns us now is: do we teach the small letters in print script and join them afterwards, or start straight away with a beautiful, flowing cursive handwriting?

Advocating print script has been associated with the idea of helping the child to recognize the similarity between the handwritten and printed word. Yet some of the lower case letters appear quite differently when printed in a book than when handwritten: for example, a vs. a ; g vs. g . Also, it is easier and more logical to recognize the letters in single formation from the experience of joined writing (from the whole to the parts) than to later have to link the letters manually. Waldorf pedagogy follows the important principle of going from the whole to the parts. If we follow this principle, we have the added bonus that cursive writing overcomes any tendency to mirror writing (e.g., d for b) which may be lingering on from the child's earlier stage of development. Cursive writing corrects this in an harmonious way. This corrective aspect is recognized by neuropsychological research.[6]

In 1916 Edward Johnston[7] was asked by the then Board of Education in the U.K. for his advice on a foundational handwriting style, but his suggestion of a running hand (cursive) was overruled by the advocates of print script. It was left to Johnston's pupil, Alfred Fairbank, to find a solution for the transition from printed letters to a running hand. He says, "Although useful for teaching infants, printed script has a serious lack as a handwriting style, for it does not develop naturally into a running hand. Accordingly some other style is taught when the child uses a pen. Print script is plainly uneconomical since it has to be abandoned and is a poor foundation for acquisition of a fundamental skill." (Note: British usage of the term infant, meaning under seven years of age.)[8]

Rhoda Kellogg in her book on children's drawings points out that most letters are made spontaneously in the young child's act of scribbling both capitals and lower case letters with the exception of G, Q, R and Y.[9] Cursive writing arises from scribbling. In order to write with a running hand, any previously learned printed letters have to be unlearned.

The latest research by Rosemary Sassoon corroborates this, pointing out that print script trains children to make an abrupt movement where all the pressure is on the finishing point at the baseline, inhibiting the flow of movement which is needed to join the letters.[10] Other researchers try to overcome this by advocating entry or exit strokes, but this still interrupts the movement flow of the hand in linking the letters naturally from their own intrinsic clockwise and anti-clockwise movement.

Professor Sassoon also suggests that it is important that handwriting is recognized as a specific skill. She proposes that teachers spend time teaching the children to understand what they are doing, introducing the terms for the structure of the letters and the correct movements for forming them, teaching the children correct pencil grasp and sitting position. Much of this is present in Waldorf methodology, though not always consistently followed.

The requirement in Waldorf pedagogy is that we take hold of the faculty of imitation which lingers on for a time after the change of teeth. This faculty we lead over into the feeling for the authority of the teacher by showing children how writing develops out of a beautiful copying of the world around them. Therefore during the first year at school, while the children are mastering the capital letters, we are also preparing the next stage, so beloved to the child, of joined up, cursive writing.

The preparation for cursive writing is the drawing of manifold patterns and the development of form drawing, which Margaret Frohlich has worked out for us from Rudolf Steiner's indications.[11] If this form drawing is a regular feature of the weekly lessons as well as a main lesson block in its own right at the commencement of the second school year, it is a natural step to the introduction of the writing of joined letters.

Rhoda Kellogg also points out that children have to perceive the difference between phonetic (linguistic) and visual (esthetic) positioning of letters.[12] In learning to write we put this perception to use. This is an important attribute needed when it comes to English spelling!

Handwriting Models and their Effects

One writes with the eye, the hand is only the organ that carries it out.[13]
—Rudolf Steiner

Every country has its own basic style of handwriting. However, we are now a "global village" as mankind has entered the time of the "conciousness soul." This stage of human development allows our ego to grasp itself as a spiritual being and to recognize this same fact in the other person. We therefore need to choose a basic handwriting form which embodies this development. The cirlce is a recognized symbol of the eternal. It also the basic form of the letters which are in daily use in the West. By consciously using an objective structure in our writing we help to free ourselves from the materialistic inductive thinking buried deep within the instincts inculcated by our present civilization. The choice of an objective form will allow the emerging individuality of each student to imprint itself on his handwriting as maturity develops.[14]

The circle is the form which most perfectly encloses space. Inner and outer are in balance. Letter forms based on the circle ◯ allow the inner space of the letter to support the outer form dynamically, preventing it from compressing the interior space which would make it hard and mean. A generous balanced inner space brings the letter form into movement and so unites the flow of the handwriting activity. A master hand is one which can also bring the inner space into movement. We can then understand what Edward Johnston intended when he spoke of creating "living letters."[15]

Pity teachers who are faced with writing on a vertical surface from a standing position! However, be consoled; the care and attention one makes in producing well-formed letters pass magically over to the children, and they are likely to excel our attempts in the end. Quiet, slow deliberation wins the day, even with our over-stimulated modern child.

Ask the children to say "o," let them feel the shape of the o with their finger. Tell them to look into their neighbor's eye and see the o form of the colored iris and its black pupil. The o sound has a warm, embracing feeling. Then ask the children what the moon does; it expands into a beautiful circle. If they look at the sun in the evening as it sinks into a cloud, they can see that it too has this circle shape. This form lends itself

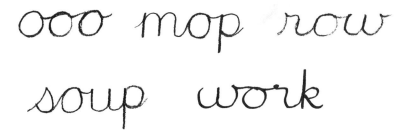

naturally to the entry and exit strokes of the other letters. It is the basic form used in professional calligraphy.

It is best to start practicing the joined writing by keeping the letters upright. Later when sequencing the letters has been mastered and the children can copy and write their own sentences, a natural slant will come of its own accord. It is best if this is not forced, as handwriting is an expression of one's own individuality.

Teachers can practice the basic round hand model on the blackboard until it feels comfortable, eliminating personal quirks in letter forms as they are writing and not allowing their handwriting to slope backwards. Taking the circle as the basic form, the body of the letters can be found with the circle, the appropriate ascender or descender can then be added. (Note that the letters m and w need two circles.) The letter f should be taught using the beautiful looped form. The letters f, i, j, l, t are made with the line stroke, but can still be written with the circle as a foundation. By working with the circle, the eye will soon school the hand to follow and balance the letter forms.[16]

It would be good if teachers read a book on graphology in order to understand the characterological effects of letter formation, remembering

that their students are still in the age of imitating what is done in front of them. Research by graphologists has found that the same traits of character shown in our handwriting are there even when writing with our foot or a tool held in another part of our body.

All children find pleasure in seeing the *whole alphabet written slowly by the teacher as one long word!* The terms for the parts of the letters can then be named: the *body* of the letters, the *ascending* and *descending* strokes, the *joining, entry,* and *exit* strokes, and the *cross bar.*

Make sure that the ascending and descending strokes are not exaggerated in length and that there are no wide spaces between the entry strokes and the body of the letter, as this makes for laborious writing and forms habits which will slow down the fluency and movement needed later when writing at speed. It is important that the loop of the letter does not obtrude into the body of the letter.

The letters can now be analyzed into families according to their structure: arched letters, cupped letters, those of the same height, those with ascenders, those with descenders and so on.

Just as the capital letters repeated the organization of the spatial movements the children mastered when learning to walk, so the small letters have the threefold structure of the child's body concealed in their

body only:

aceimnorsuvwx

cupped letters:

uvw

letters which curve over then return:

acdgoq

letters with ascenders:

bdhklt

arched letters:

mn

letters with descenders:

gjpqyz

form. The body of the letter, its center, corresponds to the rhythmic system, the center of feeling. The ascender thrusting upward, above the center, is the thinking element. The will element is called on by the descender plunging below the line on which the letter stands.

The methods described in chapter 3 for making the child dexterous, seeing that the writing activity is taken over into the whole body, can be continued in the cursive pattern (form drawing) work and in the first joined writing. Reading aloud by the class and by the individual is continued as well.

When the cursive writing stage is reached, a question which can arise is: when should a variety of writing tools be used? In many Waldorf schools it has been the custom to use colored wax stick crayons and then colored pencils until pen and ink are used. This has its drawbacks, among them time wastage and disturbance through constant breaking of the tips of the colored pencil—delightful, of course, to our students who collect these in match boxes and then spill them all over the floor—and not one is allowed to be lost either!

Happily, there is a brand of wide colored pencils now manufactured in Europe designed to meet these deficiencies.[17] When the writing instrument, such as a stick beeswax crayon, requires extra pressure, habits of tension in hand, arm, and shoulder muscles are created. Wax crayons do not glide over the surface of the paper and should be discarded for writing once the drawing of large capital letters with their correct stroke sequencing (see page 56) has been mastered. Block crayons are not suitable for any form of handwriting.

What one often observes nowadays is the lack of rhythm in children's movements and the tension and clumsiness in their handling of beeswax crayons and colored pencils. Our current situation, therefore, appears to need a medium which allows for a good rhythmic quality in writing, where an experience of weight and lightness is possible. The ordinary graphite pencil now comes back into its own, for today's modern technology has produced a plastic bonding process which makes 3B and 4B pencils that do not smudge or break so easily. These glide over the paper, and the children can have the pleasurable experience of thick and thin strokes, which with colored pencils is difficult for young children to achieve. Colored pencils can be used for decorative capital letters and titles, but the main writing should really be done in the medium which gives the best opportunity for rhythmic flow and beauty of line. It is also important for children to realize that mistakes can be corrected. Lead pencils allow this, and children can discover that rubber in erasers has another use besides Wellington (rain) boots.

It is easier and more logical for the child to recognize the letters in single formation from the experience of joined writing (the whole) than to have to link several separate letters (the parts) together. As mentioned, the idea that if the children learn to print first it will familiarize them with the printed letters in books is not a sound pedagogical concept. Of course, the majority of children can manage to learn printed letters first, but this is in contradiction to spiritual forces at work in the child's being. These forces develop into faculty, and the short term results of this process show in the poor quality of so much of today's handwriting and in a lack of sustained interest in reading.

Reading from the Printed Page

When cursive writing is established by the middle of class two, the time arrives for the children to read from printed text. Although they will have been using books at home, no doubt from the early years, and may even be reading already, the introduction to a printed book by the teacher, in the way it is presented, can have a lasting educational impression.

Books and the printed page, up to this moment, have been one of the many assorted impressions of things in the children's environment, like the kettle, knives and forks, and mealtime—part of everyday existence. Now it is to be brought to the child in its true context and purpose.

We all know that writing itself was connected with the religious life. The scribe in pre-Christian times, the monk afterwards, wrote down the Word of God. The desire for literacy in the nineteenth century really stemmed from the wish to read the Bible; for innumerable people the Bible was the first reading book. It is an important pedagogical principle that a sense for a future activity or aspect of learning is prepared in advance for the children. It is good for them to be told that when they are such and such an age, or when they come to seventh grade, then they will learn about such and such a person or subject. The children will hear stories from the Old Testament in class three. In connection with this, it is good to formally introduce the printed word from a book which stands behind all Western cultural life, the Bible. Naturally, if there are children with specific ethnic or religious backgrounds, they could be asked to bring one of their sacred texts. (One could also use the pedagogical aspect of anticipation and refer to the fact that the sacred writings from the East will be brought to the children in later classes.) This important moment should be prepared for by the teacher at a parent meeting, so that parents can also take part in feeling the importance and dignity of the moment when the printed word is placed consciously before the child. We can prepare the opening verses of Genesis with the children, or verses from the story of the Nativity. The children can learn them by heart, then write them down, before reading the text. The teacher then brings one of the larger Bibles with clear print to the classroom. One by one, children can take part in their first reading lesson, each child in turn coming to stand beside the teacher; together they point at the words as the child speaks them consciously and clearly. By choosing three or four children each morning at the beginning and end of the main lesson, all the children will have had their turn by the end of the week.

When it comes to reading, our efforts must simply be in the direction of making the child aware, this time in his head, of what has already been elaborated by the bodily forces as a whole when he was engaged in writing cursive script. Reading is then grasped mentally, because it is recognized by the child as an activity in which he has already been employed.[18]

Printing Lower Case

The printed forms of the lower case letters can be introduced in the third grade. After practicing writing these letters, the students can use them for writing poems, for example. This way of writing can be reserved for special situations in later grades. Neat printing on maps and in science books is important. The everyday writing continues to be joined cursive script.

First Pens and Ink

Finally we come to the introduction of ink in the fourth grade. This is the year when the cuttlefish, which produces its self-defensive ink, is introduced in the main lesson on natural history. Thus the curriculum itself indicates the time when the children could change to this medium for their writing. Here again we can apply the historical development approach, introducing topics appropriate to the child's developmental stage which recapitulates humankind's historical development. The latest productions of our civilization are not necessarily the best tools for the children whose bodily skills have not yet fully developed. The hard ball of the ball point pen requires it to be held too upright. It is neither pencil nor pen and destroys all the work we are doing to write rhythmically and beautifully with a relaxed penhold, and to keep these qualities when we later have to write at speed.

Pens made by the children themselves from bamboo produce excellent writing. Interest and care for their writing comes about through the experience of using something they themselves have produced, and which works! Teachers with classes of thirty or more children may quail at the thought, but it is possible with careful preparation. It is one of the means of teaching the respect for the materials of which things are made; this respect is often sadly lacking in today's children. Garden bamboo cane stakes of normal penshaft thickness are usable, cut into the usual pen holder nib shape. The pith is carefully thinned away on the nib, its width having been cut first.

Using a penknife for this activity is a good antidote to the urge to bore holes, which seems to arise in children at this age. If necessary, a reservoir to provide a flow of ink can be inserted at the back of the nib and wedged into the holder. A flexible narrow strip of copper, or a strip cut from the sealing band of a sardine can, is suitable for this. If dipping into the ink gives trouble, the reservoirs can be filled by using a paint brush as an ink filler. Teachers may like to use colored paints before they introduce ink.

Quill pens can also be made.[19] They are considered by calligraphers as unsurpassed by any other tool for writing. But free range geese will have to be found since quills are not as they were; modern farming trends have undermined their structure. Seagulls and wild turkeys are unaffected, if you can find feathers that are thick enough! Quills must be toughened by standing for a time in a solution of alum before cutting. However, as they do not last long, they can be used for special writing.

It is the use of self-made pens which enables the children to resist the urge to fall into very small writing. This urge comes after the ninth year when they, for the first time, experience themselves as individuals standing apart from the world. Before this ninth year change they have lived with the unconscious assumption that they were a part of the great world in which they live.[20] Now they feel a withdrawal from this oneness, and often overnight a child's handwriting can change from a large rhythmic style to microscopic tightness. Confidence in the world process can be regained and sustained through a right development of the art of writing.

Practical Applications and Summary
Curriculum for Handwriting in Grades 1–5

Grade One (children age 6½ to 7 years): This is the year in which writing is taught in one or two main lesson blocks each semester. Never use block crayons

- The First Semester—Preparation for Writing (See chapter 3, **pages 30–32**):

  1. Introduction of the capital letters: painting and drawing the "pictures" of the capital letters.

  2 Copying the first words and sentences: fairy tales can form the subject matter; exercise books should be as large as is compatible for the children to manage on the area of the desk or table without their slipping around, certainly not smaller than 8" x 12" (30 x 21 cm).

  3. Emphasis is on the *drawing* of the capitals. Clear letters of approximately 1½ inches (4 cm) height are best. Make sure that every child draws each stroke of the letter in its correct sequence and direction (vertical and diagonal lines above down, horizontal lines left to right). **See illustration, page 56.**

  4. See that posture, pencil grasp, distance of eyes from the paper are correct.

  5. Prepare for cursive handwriting through the drawing of cursive patterns and forms. Avoid having the running patterns straggle

across the paper; lines approximately 2 inches (5 cm) apart are helpful. The children first make the patterns between the lines quite freely. As skill increases the width of the lines can be reduced to ⅘ inch (2 ¼ cm) for the preparation of introducing the cursive hand in second grade.

- In the Middle of the School Year:

    1. Practice writing, then reading what has been written.

    2. The children can now write sentences of their own making, with the teacher's support.

    3. Continue drawing of patterns.

- In the Last Third of the School Year:

    1. The children continue writing stories and making sentences describing what they have seen and done.

    2. Introduce single lines for the writing, emphasizing good spacing and margins; make sure the work is well set out on the page.

    3. Continue form drawing; introduce graphite pencils for drawing of cursive patterns. (N.B., pencil companies using a bonding process which avoids the smudging of 3B and 4B pencils have the word "bonded" printed on the pencil shaft.)

Grade Two (children 7½ to 8 years old):   The work of this year is the teaching of a running (cursive) hand and reading.

- In the First Third of the School Year—Using pencils 3B or 4B:

    1. Introduce the cursive small letters of the alphabet (minuscules) in round hand, making the children familiar with the terms belonging to the structure of the letters. Use lines which are at least one inch apart and tell the children that the "body" of each letter rests on the line. Show how the "ascenders" and "descenders" relate to the body of the letter. The teacher may initially draw lines free-hand on the children's first pages. Liners may be helpful as the work progresses. It is important that the lines are far enough apart

so that ascenders and descenders do not get tangled up. A proper contrast between letter spacing and word spacing should be seen.

2. Spend time on the details and teach the careful use of the eraser. How many of today's children see erasers being used by adults? Teaching is necessary. We can do this best by sitting beside him and talking to the eraser, commenting on it, "Mm, you are a soft one; this one is hard. We shall have to use you very lightly or you'll leave a smudge behind."

3. Speak about the paper, its surface, the whiteness: "I wonder where the tree grew that you came from?" Of yellowish paper, one could say, "That must be paper that has already done a lot of work! It's made from recycled paper."

4. Present material to the children as a picture of your reactions, your judgment and experience, not as information of how they are made. That comes later and will be of a more lasting interest to them if you have prepared them in this way first.

5. Is the pencil hold/grasp correct and is the left hand doing its support work? Again, check posture of trunk, shoulders, neck, head. Use flexible and supportive pencil grips for students whose grasp on the pencil is tense or awkward. There are pencil grips that fit both left- and right-handed people.[21]

6. When introducing the cursive minuscules (lower case letters), help the children to discover, from the stroke directions and the invisible movements between them, how the capital letters have shrunk to their new shape. For example, E e, H h. Write the whole alphabet as one long "word." Have the children find the new forms which the capital letters have received in this long cursive word and in the sentences they write. Practice writing the alphabetical sequence in groups of three (*illustration a*), and in reverse (*illustration b*). Emphasize the beauty of the looped form of f in *illustration c*, never as *illustration d*, a very common evasion of keeping the loops correctly both on the same side of the ascender and descender. (*Illustration d* is actually ss—occasionally used in old German formal writing.) Repeat such practice sequences, increasing the number of letters: *illustration e*. The teacher can speak the names of the letters as she writes each one; the children

then whisper as they copy them, until each child can write them with his eyes shut.

7. Remember to personalize as you describe how these lower case letters should be formed. "Notice that I'm making a *d*. Over goes the circle and back, up goes the ascender, not too high. We don't

illustration a

abc cde efg

illustration b

zyx xuw

illustration c   **illustration d**

f   *f*

illustration e

abcdefg ghijklmn

want something to get tangled in it. See how the exit stroke cuddles up to the circle (*o*) and its exit stroke makes a straight line to the *g*, with just enough space for a bird to sit on before it is chased away by a *dog*!"

8. The children read from their writing, learning to recognize the short sounds of the vowels, the letter-sound combinations.[22]

- The Second Third of the School Year:

1. The children continue copying, writing, and making their own sentences.

2. Introduce the first printed books. When this is done we should lay the foundation for a recognition of the beauty of printed letters. We cannot do better than to have in our classroom examples of the ideal letters, those that have influenced all Western writing—the Trajan capitals remaining on the columns of his triumphal arch (Roman Emperor Trajan, AD 98–117). Edward M. Catich has produced each of these letters on separate cards printed in a terracotta that exactly matches the coloring of the Roman tiles of this period. The children can thus see letters as an artistic creation in and of themselves.[23] If you cannot write calligraphy yourself, ask your high school art teacher to write out poems and paragraphs in formal calligraphy for your classroom. Invite him/her to do one in front of the class, so the children can see the care taken.

- The Last Third of the School Year:

1. Writing and reading practice continues together with form drawing.

2. Give exercises for sleepy children, nervously awake children, those with poor speech/movement coordination, etc. (see text).

Grade Three

- Printing of lower case letters can be introduced, getting ready for neat labeling on maps and in science books in the following grades.

- Introduce a variety of capital letters for cursive writing.[24]

By permission from *Form Drawing* by Margaret Frohlich and Hans Niederhauser:

third grade

fourth grade   *fifth grade*

- For practice use the "pink books" developed by Else Göttgens for practice of cursive writing with correct sizing; these books have a soft tone of colors to guide the sizing of the writing. There are also other similar handwriting practice books.[25]

- The writing of business letters provides for the teaching of space and layout. Each business letter can be presented as a picture in itself. Writing business letters can continue in the later grades, in grammar lessons for instance. The inculcate strucutre, form, and consciousness of content.

- Besides Old Testament stories, making up, telling, and solving riddles provide material for writing.

- For children who shrink their writing to quite small letters, it is useful to draw freehand "paths" for them to write within. If a student writes too large the same approach may be used. See illustrations below.

Grade Four

- The children can write with sticks in sand or earth, then make their own writing implements from bamboo or quill (see text) to use with ink (or paint). Next, you can introduce dipping pens before the fountain pens.

- Consult books on handwriting for correct angle of pen to paper, type of nib for chosen style of writing, e.g., an upright round hand, a sloping round hand (see Bibliography). Choose a fountain pen with care.

- Introduce a variety of cursive writing styles, using the fountain pens for slow and careful writing. See "Teachers, Look to Your Handwriting" in *Learning Difficulties: A Guide for Teachers* for guidance in creatively introducing cursive script according to temperaments.[26] This will aid the children in coming to their own style of writing over time.

Grade Five

- Give opportunity for children to use a variety of pens, including felt tip, roller ball (not ballpoint as this easily leads to an excess of pressure onto the paper), mapping pens, and different nib types.

- An infallible guide when reviewing lesson preparation is to ask oneself these questions: "Have I gone from the whole to the part?" and "Have I activated the soul capacities of thinking, feeling, and willing?" But BEWARE: children, until approximately seven years old, experience this sequence in reverse—from the will to feeling to thinking. For the age group of seven to fourteen years, there is a shift in the sequence. The center of these three faculties now becomes the dominant one—from feeling to will and thinking. Because the feeling life now predominates, we need to start with the *image* for the content of the lesson, appealing to the forces of sympathy and antipathy—*feeling*, then *practicing* what has been introduced—the will. This accomplished, we can call on the recognition of what has been learnt, thus addressing the developing thinking consciousness. Through following the body and soul development, we enable the three basic capacities of the human being to become a faculty of objective perception when the individual reaches maturity.

First artistic forms, thence the transition to drawings, thence to writing and so by degrees to printing.[27]

—Rudolf Steiner

Grade One:

SUN EARTH AND AIR

Grade Two:

have wrought with God's care

Grade Three:

that the plants live and bear.

The writing can diminish in size in later classes with introduction of fine nibs, etc. Printing as in the last example above should only be practiced for poems and special paragraphs; normal cursive handwriting continues in main lesson books.

Written by a fourth grade girl:

This is an example of my best handwriting.
In first grade I learned to print. In
second grade I learned cursive. In
third grade I learned cursive capitals.*

* The drawing/printing of Roman capital letters.

Sixth grade girl physics block:

DARK AND LIGHT

When you are in a dark room, you feel enclosed.
I also think that we had to move, so that we could make
sure of where we were. My class had this experience.

CHAPTER 6

OH, SPELLING!

*Spelling lessons must run parallel with developing the children's feelings of
respect and esteem for what their predecessors have established.*[1]

—Rudolf Steiner

We only need to spell when we are writing. When developed as a
capacity, spelling must not in any way intrude into consciousness; it must
be entirely the servant of thought. The faculty of inner visualization
must be working at a subconscious level, having developed out of the
capacity of the sense of self-movement which we have been using in our
teaching method. (See previous chapters)

It has already been described how movement, speaking, and thinking
develop out of each other.[2] All three of these processes are involved in
spelling.

On the other hand, spelling itself has had its own evolution and has
only become static comparatively recently. With the loss of interest in
the Greek and Latin languages, words have suffered from a separation
from their own ancestry; their sound and spelling are no longer evoca-
tive of the past. Thus the teacher stands in the classroom with little
inner connection himself with words as history, only as tools for communication, and this emptiness works upon the children, producing a
lack of interest.[3] This, in turn, affects the child's will and its power on
the recall of memory. Conventional teaching of spelling does not really
reach to the root of the situation. Some children manage to learn by rote
but, like other capacities, for instance, arithmetic or music, either one
can spell or one can't. There are some children who are naturally good
at spelling and some who are unable to retain the visual picture of the

word however many times they write it. They may have learned it correctly, but under the stress of writing at speed, the old faulty picture returns. This puts the responsibility on the teacher to articulate the sounds in each word and their syllables correctly: peel, table, melody, international, reverberate. Also, clarity at the end of words: *wall*, not, *waw*; *world*, not, *worl*, as is so often heard. This brings into focus the emphasis on the training of the speech organs which Rudolf Steiner required of teachers. He gave specific speech exercises for this purpose, providing for every need as long ago as the 1920s.[4]

Visual and Auditory Spelling

The visual learner, who learns best through the sense of sight, may notice the overall shape (outline) that a word has—

and will remember this shape, but may not recollect if the ascending stroke came from k, h, d, etc. nor if the descender was from g, j, p, etc. To discriminate between these he needs to inwardly hear the sounds of the letters (auditory discrimination). It is helpful to teach these visual children alphabetical spelling by telling them the names of the letters in each word. Encourage them to whisper the name of the letter as they write. They, particularly, benefit from being shown how to use a dictionary.

Auditory discrimination is educated by exact articulation and enunciation. Lack of clarity in the teacher's pronunciation—*effect* or *affect*? *tendency* or *tendancy*? *ndure*: is that *an-* or *en-*dure? does not lay a good foundation for spelling nor help to overcome poor speaking habits imitated from the children's environment. The non-hearing of the vowels, and their fine differentiation, can be bound up with the emotional life which is adversely affected by, for instance, lack of proper attention from the adults in a young child's life (neglect). A study of the child's case history may reveal possible causes, such as the young child's having been exposed to frequent changes of busy caregivers while the single mother worked full-time. Early ear infections or allergies which cause fluid build-up in the middle ear can also affect the young child's hearing of similar sounding vowels and consonants. It is during the early years while the child is intently listening to the variety of sounds in the mother tongue that the foundation is laid for later auditory discrimination. Nursery rhymes, ditties, songs, rhythmical verses, and poems are important for developing and healing this capacity to discern the sounds of our language. Thus the early childhood oral tradition has a very important educational purpose.[5]

The visual memory of each child needs training. Caught, fought: these and other eccentricities of the English language need to be taught, reviewed, and practiced. A way of training this ability is to draw a simple form on the blackboard. The teacher tells the class to look at it while ten is being counted; then it is erased. The next morning the children take out their practice books and try to draw the form from memory. Here we are using the subconscious forces at work in sleep, and are engaging the will through the visual recall. To strengthen the auditory memory we could use pronunciation verses such as those given in *Phonic Rhyme Time* by Mary Nash-Wortham,[6] a speech therapist who has grappled with such problems for many years.

In general, it is best not to allow children to make spelling mistakes, as this engraves the error onto the memory and into the movement system. This may mean putting a weaker speller to the left side of a good speller (if this latter child is a right-hander), allowing him to copy his neighbor rather than make errors.

Another example for working on spelling is to make a short graphic sentence containing two words which need implanting into memory and write this sentence on the blackboard. Then, following the analyzing method (whole to parts), let different children read the sentence, then the chosen word, then its letters. Next the sentence is concealed, and a child is asked to spell the word, another to come to the blackboard and write it. The following day the children stand with their backs towards the blackboard and, in turn, different children are asked to say the sentence; others are asked to say the fourth word, then the sentence; others to say the last word in the sentence and to name the second letter in that word, etc. The children can then turn and read the sentence. The third day the children can be asked to insert words/letters that have been erased, then to write the sentence from memory. Naturally a new sentence can be added in succeeding days in classes of older children.

Remedies for Spelling Problems

Using such methods we can implement the three-day rhythm in our teaching, to which Rudolf Steiner has drawn our attention.[7] This rhythm takes into account the threefold structure of the soul with its developing capacities and the importance of the intervals of sleep. We have to give the opportunity for the full assimilation of our subject matter into the soul-bodily organization before calling on the child to reproduce it in his intellect.

Spelling corrections are a problem to both teacher and students, especially if the work is well written and comes back defaced with red marks and—whisper it only—sometimes a teacher's scribble/messy handwriting!

It has a beneficial consoling effect on children of all ages if the teacher sits down beside a student, consciously places himself in the correct posture for writing, and slowly and beautifully writes out three or four of the misspelled words for him to copy—once! We cannot do this every day for every child, but we can see to it that in every main lesson block we have written once in each child's book in his presence. Watching the care with which the teacher treats words awakens interest and conscience towards them.

We also need to recognize "original" spellers. In the heat of composition writing, they feel the picture-meaning sense of the sounds as they write with the rhythm and the content of their thought, and consequently spell the same word in two or three different ways, characteristic, by the way, of spelling before Dr. Johnson started work on his dictionary published in 1755.[8] Correct spelling gradually came into being after that. To force these children to learn spelling is the best way to turn them into bad spellers, for having learned how to spell words out of their context, they never know which is right when these words are required—what they imagine or the correction. For them, and truly for all poor spellers, it is far better to comment at the end of their compositions that they have spelled *accommodation* and *necessary* correctly rather than to return their work to them scored with red lines.

It is the "bizarre" speller who is our problem. She puts any old letters together, for example, *and* as *nda*, *the* as *teh*, *help* as *pleh*, *was* as *wsa*. When we see this kind of spelling, even when copying, remedial help on a one-to-one basis is necessary. Until this can be arranged we must concentrate on her writing, making her copy out most beautifully a line from a poem which the class is learning, a verse or a sentence with alliterated sounds. This is the best way to help her and also the original speller.

The "kinesthetic" learner, who learns best by engaging the senses of touch, self-movement, and balance, benefits from writing words with large gestures.[9] She can write the word(s) in cursive: writing with chalk (or a wet sponge) on the blackboard; with the right foot (for right-handers), a crayon or pencil held between the big and second toes, on large paper on the floor; writing in sand with the toes; writing with the fingertips tracing the word(s) on the desk; followed by writing the word(s) large with a smooth flowing graphite pencil or felt tip pen on a large piece of (butcher) paper. She can also walk the shape of the cursive letters on the floor. To help her picture these forms inwardly (inner visualization) while moving them, she faces the same direction (rather than following her nose) as she walks the forms of the letters as if her walking feet were writing on the floor; simultaneously she speaks their sounds. Another movement approach to spelling is to have the student step forward as he spells out each letter, then step backward while spelling the word backwards, stepping simultaneously with speaking each letter name. These kinesthetic approaches are also helpful for the more visual and auditory learners. Such methods may be used as soon as spelling is being taught and afterwards for all ages.

There is a large body of work contributed by teachers to help the poor spellers. The learning of specially selected groups of words is the main consideration here. We can use the everlasting sequence of at, cat, mat. Taking a word and adding blends and suitable prefix and suffix: at, cat, scratch, scratching, scratched. There is certainly a short time between eight and nine years of age when children love collecting, and this moment can be used for such work. But when this is over, time spent on learning by rote can be a sterile procedure, and it would be better used in the work of a remedial nature which arouses the whole of the child's abilities, rather than concentrating on his intellectual memory only.

Other Approaches for Spelling Problems

Painting, for instance, can be used to help poor spellers and readers, not in extra painting lessons but in the usual weekly one. Painting is not to be regarded as a subject but as a part of everyday life; that is why Rudolf Steiner made the class teachers responsible for it instead of having it taught by an art teacher. Social training in the class also consists of the children's recognizing that each one has some special need, and they must accept that Tom is different from Will, and that Mary has to have something which Sally does not.

If we have noticed that there is a vague and sleepy child who cannot take hold of her thoughts, then in the weekly painting lesson for the class we have her paint two or three geometrical forms, one superimposed upon the other. She then has to learn to see which parts the forms have in common and which will protrude   This helps her to differentiate in her inner looking (inner visualization). Another exercise is to paint a background color leaving a chosen geometrical form as a blank space in the center, which can then be painted in with a complementary color. Here we call on the child's ability to hold a picture in her mind and not let it become washed away by the too strong processes at work in her body. After working at such exercises, words may be substituted for the forms.

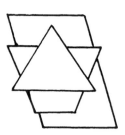

Painted freehand forms

Learning difficulties can be foreseen by accurate observation, especially if we have taught the same children in the first three grades, i.e., before nine years of age. Rudolf Steiner gives particular ways of painting for children who hold on to their thoughts and so become "overloaded" with them, as well as for those children whose thoughts disappear into the depths of the body.[10] In the first case, three to four *contrasting* colors are painted in large areas next to each other: red, blue, yellow or green, orange, violet. This has an effect similar to the relief we have when gazing out over a landscape. In the second (opposite) situation, *colors which blend* with one another should be used and painted next to each other with a drawing style in narrow, ribbon-like forms, several colors together looped over and under each other: blue, green, yellow or red, orange, yellow. Here the child's consciousness is not allowed to go on dreaming in her bodily processes; in this exercise she must remember to lift her brush to go over or under the loops. She has to wake up just as she does on a busy road. Steiner follows this by illustrating how the same pedagogical remedy can be extended into the gym lesson by seeing that the second type of children alternates the gymnastic exercises with reciting and singing, while the other children remain silent between the exercises.

Thus the subject matter of lessons can be used both to heal and to bring out latent faculties. The teachers must have really observed the children in their care to understand how, by using the conjunction of body and soul working together, the intellectual intelligence will be brought forth as a fruit in due season.

Practical Applications and Summary

- The clarity and pronunciation of the teacher's speech is important.[11] This is especially vital for children with weak visual memory.

- For auditory and visual memories, look at possible emotional interferences. (See text.)

- Use the three-day rhythm for teaching spelling. **(See page 86.)**

- Explore types of spelling difficulties.

- If available, use one or more of the following texts (or similar texts): *The Oxford Spelling Dictionary, Dolch: Sight Word Activities, Spelling Teachers Book of Lists, The Scholastic Dictionary of Spelling: Over 5,000 Words.* Teachers in the U.K., Australia, and New Zealand may have access to Schonell's classic publication, *Essentials in Teaching and Testing Spelling.*[12]

- "Rainbow books," as suggested by Else Göttgens, longtime Waldorf teacher and consultant, are notebooks containing pages in different (rainbow) colors; in these the child "collects" sight words according to spelling, not sound. Each letter combination gets a color, so the *ei* words receive, weigh, neighbor, their, either, etc., may be written on a pale yellow page, while the *ie* words friend, piece, pliers, sieve, shield, etc., may be collected on a blue page. Children like to collect things, and in the rainbow book they collect words which cannot be sounded out phonetically.[13]

- A book of puzzles with other activities such as Gillian Aitken's *Spotlight on Words* may be of help for the 10–13 year-olds.[14]

- Use Steiner's specific exercises for children who loose their thoughts and those who cannot let go of their thoughts.[15]

- A good exercise for reversal problems is form drawing in a palindrome, i.e., mirroring across vertical and horizontal lines (third grade and up).[16]

- All spatial dimensions are contained in the spiral. When drawing spiral forms, the soul faculties corresponding to each spatial dimension are activated. The symmetry/sagittal plane, which separates left from right in us, is connected to the soul faculty of thinking. The frontal plane, separating front from behind, is related to our will. And the horizontal plane, separating above from below, is related to our feeling life.[17] See chapter 3.

CHAPTER 7

WRITING DIFFICULTIES

Our rightful place as educators is to be removers of hindrances.[1]

Each child in every age brings something new into the world from divine regions, and it is our task as educators to remove bodily and psychical obstacles out of his way; to remove hindrances so that his spirit may enter in full freedom into life.[2]

—Rudolf Steiner

Written by a 10-year-old boy struggling with his writing:

> The sun rses in the East
> waking man and flower ant beast.
> The sun sinks in west

Posture

The causes of many of the obstacles which children encounter when learning handwriting can be traced to hindrances in their development during the first seven years of life. As the young child's movements develop from lying on his back to grasping, rolling, crawling, creeping, standing, and walking, his postural system matures. A mature postural system allows the child to develop and maintain good standing, walking, sitting, and working posture, as well as to grasp and use his pencil in a relaxed way. This maturation process involves the basic senses of touch, life, self-movement, and balance. The organs of perception for these senses are nerve receptors in skin, internal organs, muscles, tendons, and joints and in the inner ear. These senses mature as the young child moves freely through space, using his own efforts and unhampered by contraptions like walkers or restrictions imposed by overanxious caregivers. Neuropsychology has an extensive range of research on the problems caused by lack of integration of the postural system.[3]

If we look at the skeleton and the muscles interlaced by the nervous system, we find that the general plan is similar for the body of every human being. The ratio of our bones one to another approaches the golden mean.[4] Whether we have large or small bones, it is this skeletal structure which enables us to become vertical to the surface of the earth, and this is the foundation for the spatial perception described in the first chapter. Each brain, too, has the same composition; if each were different there would be no brain surgery as we know it today. The same applies to the position of our organs. Fortunately surgeons do not have to explore our body to find our liver or our heart; they know exactly where they are positioned and how they function. Our physical body has, during long periods of evolution, developed into this marvelous, complex organization which is now the pattern, the archetype, for humanity over the whole earth. As Keith Critchlow and Jon Allen observe in relation to architectural design considerations:

> The human body is held as the standard of wholeness and significance, in fact the perfected system in such widely separate societies as the ancient Chinese, the Indian Vedic sagas, the fourteenth century Brotherhood of Purity as well as in the better known Christian Gospels. . . . Even reduced to a functional standard and described as ergonomics, the human body is still the standard. . . . The psychology of the body permeates physiology in the same way that the nervous system permeates all the tissues.[5]

It is this archetypal body of bones, muscles, and nerves that is the concern of the science of neuropsychology which has developed during this century from the work of Sir Charles Sherrington.[6] The unification of this complex organism we call our physical body is mirrored back to us from the brain. This composite picture gives us the possibility to say "I," and because all other persons are likewise composed, we recognize them as "you." We see the individuality of each person expressed in appearance and in the way he uses this archetype.

Early Movement Responses

The I-awareness gradually awakens at definite intervals during childhood and is mirrored among other things in the first scribbles and drawn forms which are made by the child.[7] In order to use a pencil or any tool—stick, spoon, etc.—most children need to have integrated the early movement responses (primal reflexes) which have supported the body in the womb and during the first months after birth.[8] By freely going through the innate developmental movement stages, the infant and young child move with more and more ease and coordination. The earliest reflexive movements are thus replaced by more mature, controlled motion. In other words, the early movements are "integrated" into the nervous system.

In March 1993, Jane Field, a practicing neuro-developmental therapist, presented a paper entitled "A Vicious Circle" in Chester, U.K. to the fifth European Conference on Neuro-developmental Delay in Children with Specific Learning Difficulties.[9] Among many causes of learning challenges, she highlighted the drugs which are given to mothers during childbirth; these can affect the oxygen supply to the brain of the baby during this crucial time. She describes several primal reflexes which belong to the embryonic and neonatal periods and which are normally integrated into the infant's nervous system through his spontaneous movements during the early months of his life. Subtle remnants of these primal reflexes create immature movement patterns which can continue to interfere with the movements which a school-aged child intends to make. The child's movements are then uncoordinated, and writing is usually a painful experience. Physical therapists and occupational therapists also contribute to our understanding of movement development. They alert us to the fact that these remaining immature movement patterns can become obstacles to the child's developing movement skills, causing excess tension, poor coordination, and a delay in motor development.[10]

Only those primal reflexes not fully integrated at the appropriate time, which give rise to immature movement patterns and which therefore interfere specifically with the skill of handwriting, will be described here. They are the asymmetric tonic neck reflex (ATNR) and the symmetric tonic neck reflex (STNR) or (TNR). The vertical midline barrier, though not considered a reflexive movement response, is included as well.

The asymmetric tonic neck reflex is usually active from birth to about three to eight months. It functions when the head is turned to one side which causes the arm on that side to stretch out while the other arm bends; often the legs repeat the same movements, one stretches while the other bends. In the classroom we may see movement patterns, which develop from a subtle retention of this reflex, if we look at the sitting position which the child uses as he writes.[11] He often sits on his left leg or draws it back to wrap around the chair leg; the left arm is bent on the desk and often his head is lowered to the arm as he writes. He pushes his paper to the top or to the right of the desk so the writing hand is stretched out as far as possible. Needless to say he is not popular with his neighbor for usurping his space in this way! (See illustration page 34.)

The symmetric tonic neck reflex is seen when the infant, just beginning to stand on hands and knees, lifts his head up, causing him to extend his arms and bend his legs, so he ends up sitting on his legs. Conversely, if the head is bent forwards he will bend his arms and stretch his legs, ending up on his stomach. Try placing yourself in the position of looking up at the blackboard and you can see the problems the child has in the classroom when this reflex is only partially integrated.[12] The child sits with the paper pushed forward to the far edge of the desk, with his legs drawn in under the chair, feet and lower legs gripping the chair legs for balance. Because of the tension he has to exert to maintain his posture, he continually looses his place as he lifts his head up to see the text on the blackboard, then lowers it to copy the words into his book.

The vertical midline barrier is not integrated until later; usually by the time the child is seven it has been fully integrated. This barrier is an invisible wall down the center of the body; it is there in the young child in order to enable both the left and the right side of the body to develop. The young child picks up the object on his right with the right hand and the object on his left with his left hand. He does not easily cross over. Watch a small boy flying his toy plane, holding it in his right or left hand. When he wants to fly it across his body, he switches it to his other hand at the midline, in order to continue its journey. As this midline barrier is often present until the child is between six and seven years, parents may assume that the child is left-handed when they notice this use of the left hand, even though it is actually used in alternation with the right. Therefore they may not encourage a more consistent use of the right hand, for example, always opening a door with the right hand, putting the right arm first into the right sleeve of a coat, and so on. Many children are thus left in an ambidextrous condition which is not always to their advantage. Retention of this midline barrier leads the child to position his paper on the far side of his desk so that it is over to one side of the midline. Reading is often a problem as the eyes may jerk when crossing the midline; this makes the eyes return to read the next line below or to the beginning of the same line. In order to achieve speed with legible handwriting we need the integration of the motor and sensory organization.[13]

Hindrances to Handwriting: Some of their Origins

Now let us consider some of the everyday occurrences which work against the natural development of the senses and the skills which they control. As early as the first main lesson at school, it will be apparent to the class teacher which children are experiencing hindrances, both to mastering their bodies and to the harmonious flow of their will forces.

Many factors play into this. A very common one is that in the years before the change of teeth (birth to seven) the inherited body has been too hardened so that it is difficult to transform into a vehicle for the expression of the child's own will; the habit patterns of the family are so embedded in the child's constitution that the work of the individual's soul-spirit on the bodily constitution is hampered (see chapter 1).

The polar opposite of this hardening is the case in which the bodily constitution is delicate and mobile, while the environment is harsh and over-stimulates the nervous system; again the work of the soul-spirit of the child is interfered with and the life forces are depleted. Both these conditions will produce many warning signs which show that the child is unable to absorb the content of a lesson and change it into the necessary faculty. We will consider some of the signs and make suggestions for overcoming them.

Another common complaint is lack of concentration; this complaint is made both by teachers and parents. A common cause for this is too many sense impressions crowding in on the children as soon as they wake up. What is the first thing that they see on waking? The wall paper! Is it strongly patterned and colored with cartoon figures or complicated forms? This can be an irritant to a delicate nervous system, and even to a strong one! A plain wall in a warm color (subtle pink and orange tones) is more health-giving to the senses; it can be enhanced by curtains of a deeper shade. Is the radio on when they wake? Is it audible over the whole house? Is the morning news on at breakfast when Father is reading the newspaper and Mother talking about the arrangements for the day? Today we can add the effect which video and computer games have on the children's concentration and the resulting fatigue and irritability. Is it any wonder that teachers complain that children just don't hear what is said to them?

In these conditions the vitality and delicacy of perception of the senses of sight and hearing are already overstimulated by the time children arrive at school, and if they come in cars driven at high speed, with the radio on too, how can we expect young children to settle down to quiet, concentrated work with the residue of all these impressions working from the sense organization onto the soul? Children arriving by school bus are not in a much better condition. They have usually worked each other up into a state of excitement. Even the effects of the healthy walk to school are depleted when there is constant heavy traffic on the road. All this the teacher has to take into account. Therefore, to spend ten minutes on a simple painting exercise or shaded color drawing before the morning verse would go a long way in helping children to settle down to work.[14]

Another more subtle and deeper cause of lack of concentration is the child's having his play constantly interrupted. Overly anxious or dominant parents or caregivers may be unintentionally disturbing the young child. Some caregivers may not recognize that the child has a fantasy working in the will which wants to develop a particular kind of play interest. The child may be one who is slow at starting his play, and, just as he has become immersed in it, the caregiver comes along with something else that needs to be done or to change his place of play. This background accounts for many a fidgety child. The teacher can distinguish this cause through careful observation, tactful questions about the child's childcare situations, and by visiting the home. As a remedy for this, the teacher will make sure that the child has an opportunity to play himself out, either in the classroom, or even by arranging a time when the child (if he is in the first grade) could join with the kindergarten. These children are often so frustrated that they are glad to be with younger children, who become their healers.[15]

Two other obstacles to good work, which have to be tackled, are incessant talking and an inability to remember. These may come more from the soul-spirit of the child than from the environment. Observation may show that the breathing of these children is very shallow. This can be helped through working with the child's body, in this way making the child more active in his soul nature. Rudolf Steiner has emphasized in his educational lectures the unique condition that, when the children are between the ages of the change of teeth and puberty, what is done with the body works on the soul. Conversely, if we make the child active in his soul-feeling life, this works back onto his bodily constitution.[16] We need to remember that this law, the result of spiritual scientific research, works in both positive and negative ways. As educators we have usually to deal with the negative results of this law; we must also use it to help the child's condition become a healthy one!

This we can do in the main lesson by using rhythmic activities whenever possible: chanting times tables to clapping and stepping, walking forward and backward when counting. The especially dreamy or sluggish child can take very large steps. Their stepping rhythm could be on every third step: 1, 2, **3**, 4, 5, **6**, while the other children take regular, even steps, emphasizing every other step: 1, **2**, 3, **4**, 5, **6**. This is the way we can individualize in group activities. These dreamy children need also to live in strong feelings, and we should see that in our telling of stories we prepare some incident or characterization with them particularly in mind, directing our attention to them when speaking. The individualization in painting lessons as already described in Chapter 6 is also necessary. These are examples of body-soul hindrances to the faculty we are educating. Now we will consider deeper physiological difficulties.

Coordination

The prevalent hindrance which teachers need to be alert to is the lack of coordination. This will have shown itself in the children when the teachers have used the methods of teaching we have been describing. The natural faculty of coordination is there in normal children when they have been allowed to develop at their own pace in the vital first eighteen months of life. It is important, for example, that parents or caregivers have allowed the child to use his own strength to lift himself into the sitting and vertical positions and to take his first steps out of his own volition. We work against this natural development if walking is practiced while holding the child. This delays and retards his progress and the development of his will forces. Walking aids (walkers) and baby bounce apparatus may be convenient to the adult and seemingly enjoyed by the child, but they interfere with the delicate coordination development in the child, particularly with the integration of the postural system. Holding infants under their arms so as to prop their feet onto the seated parent's legs to encourage standing also interferes with their movement development. The results only show themselves in subsequent periods of development.

Another hindrance to the development of good coordination is too much help with too much hurry. Here the child is often denied the freedom to master the primary skills which he needs, like managing his food. First the skill of using his fingers—too early enforcement of spoons and forks can interfere with developing fine motor (finger) coordination. The child wants to explore his food with his sense of touch first and then taste what he is going to eat, to stir the piece of bread in his milk with his finger and enjoy seeing it float. How much nicer it tastes when you have made it part of your experience of sight and movement, and it really doesn't matter if it goes in your ear before your mouth. After all it is only comparatively recently that you have had a mouth! This is difficult to condone by parents who have been very strictly brought up themselves. Their own attitudes are influenced by the memory of the authority of their own upbringing which, alas, easily overcomes their own spontaneous pleasure and enjoyment in experiencing how their baby finds his way into life. This very enjoyment can rouse guilty feelings which end up with the baby's being fed by the mother or father and by their helping to dress and button up his coat, tie his shoe laces, put on his gloves—all fascinating exploring experiences for the child if he gets a chance to have them. If he has too much help, then he learns to behave as a will-less lump while the caregiver pushes and pulls. There is the other situation, where the child struggles with his tasks, but his will is continually thwarted by someone intervening and doing quickly what the child is trying to do. Bad temper, confusion, and, in the end, superficiality can result.

All this kind of treatment retards the child's will from living and working in his growing body. Some of the consequences are clear in what is now designated as cross dominance and laterality problems. These show themselves in the classroom as ambidextrous tendencies and a lack of handedness skills, conditions which may be recognized in themselves, but unfortunately not in the context of daily life.

Dominance[17]

Let us now consider some basic terms. *Dominance* is the preference we have for the use of one side of our body. For the majority of us it is our right side, our right eye, right ear, right nostril, right side of the jaw, right hand and right foot. Eye dominance is not necessarily determined by the quality of our vision, as there is sometimes the complicated situation where the vision of the non-dominant eye is better than that of the dominant one. Dominance is a picture of how the soul has taken up its abode in the body, of its freedom to move and be in command of the instrument of its will.

Laterality is the term for general alignment of dominance. There is *cross laterality* (or *cross dominance*) when one or other of the members of the opposite side is stronger and takes precedence with its skill. We may then have a left eye dominance in a right-handed and right-footed child or a left foot dominance in a right-handed and right-eyed child. The preference pattern may even go back and forth from one side to the other—left eye, right hand, left foot, or right eye, left hand, right foot. When preference for one hand has not been established (*unconfirmed dominance*), this may be mistaken for ambidextrousness, and the indiscriminate use of either hand is allowed to set into a habit. True *ambidextrousness* is the condition in which both hands have the same level of skill, as much dextrousness in each hand for craft work as for writing. There may also be unconfirmed dominance of the feet, where the child chooses either foot for hopping, kicking, stamping, or balancing on.

It is easy to see that children who have these physiological conditions are going to have problems when writing and reading are required of them, especially when it is required at the early age that our general educational system demands. These demands then come at an age when the body has not yet completed its development, and the skills which the children need are not yet fully prepared.

And what are these skills? Up to the 1930s, and decidedly so in earlier generations, many of these skills were developed in helping mother and imitating her activities while she was doing her housework and cooking. Sweeping floors is an excellent way of crossing the vertical midline and developing laterality; washing and wringing clothes calls on coordinating left and right, working at the vertical midline and developing hand preference—not to mention stirring cakes and beating eggs. Dusting—lifting the vase with the left hand and dusting underneath it with the right hand—soon settles ambidextrousness if the children are allowed to go around with their own duster and copy mother. Boys had their share of practical activities, and when all else failed there was always the possibility of watching a man digging a hole in the road. Then there were the endless games, seasonal ones and those of everyday vintage, from "Here We Go Round the Mulberry Bush" (washing, combing, stamping through all the parts of the body), to "Five Stones" or "Jacks," which exercise so wonderfully the movement relationship between the radius and the ulna (bones of the forearm), bringing the child's will forces right down to the fingertips.

All these activities which make the body skillful are undergoing a slow death. In their place comes a fixing of the gaze as the eyes are held by the glare of the TV set (or computer screen) or as the road disappears under the wheels of the car. The constant kicking of balls, the mechanical movement of hands and feet, the fixed grip of the bike handles and the fast revolving feet underneath, all these seemingly active (yet mechanical) pursuits lead to the over-development of one part of the body. Too much too soon can lead to trouble ahead unless parents provide proper compensation and balance for this. Alas, even our helpful practical domestic devices work against the natural soul developments of our children. The new fold-up strollers, a boon to a shopping parent, turn the toddler's gaze away from the parent to constantly changing objects and unknown people. Missing is the kind of conversation and interaction that the parent would have with the child if he were sitting so he faces the parent who is pushing him along in the stroller. Children referred for speech therapy are often those who have not been conversed with sufficiently in the early years. The loss of the constant sight of what is rightly the central perception in the child's existence, the mother, in exchange for a succession of fleeting pictures which he cannot yet conceptualize, has repercussions in the depth of his soul life. As adults we have to use what our practically oriented culture provides, but we have also the obligation to recognize its effects and make, out of our own initiative, suitable compensations.

When this has not been done, the teacher has to face the results. He will have in his class children who will pick up the pencil with their left hand and pass it to the right hand, showing there is a weakness in the establishment of right-handedness, or children who turn their drawing paper around and around when they are drawing, so that the object does the moving, not the eye and the hand. There is the fierce grip on the pencil, sometimes with the fingers sliding down until they are almost covering the pencil point, the finger joints that are bent backward, or the ballpoint pen held in a too upright position. We see hands that are held at the edge of the desk instead of letting its surface support the forearms of the writing and supporting hands. No wonder the children tire easily with the pull of the muscles forcing them to twist themselves into bad sitting positions. As for the writing itself, if we are watchful we shall notice the children writing s and e from the bottom up and the numbers 2, 4, 5, 6 and 9 as well! Double o's are sometimes written as clockwise circular loops ⟳⟳ while capital E is made with the strokes starting at the bottom and the horizontal strokes moving toward the initial stroke! How do we find the right correction for these signals of distress?

The Will Senses

Edward M. Catich, an American calligrapher (see Biographies), describes the sense needed for comfortable writing as "kinesthesis" which is, he says, like the five exteroceptive senses (seeing, hearing, smelling, tasting, temperature sense), a true sense. Kinesthesis, as Edward Catich defines it, is the term for the sense, while kinesthesia is the conscious learning activity of this kinesthetic sense.

> One does not have to look at any part of one's body to know whether the muscles are contracted, or joints bent, or that the body is in a particular posture or action; for example, if with my eyes shut I trace with my finger a figure 8, I am able to know that it is a figure 8 that my finger has traced. And if I wish to sign my name in the dark, I am able to do so because constant practice in

the muscular action of making my signature has established in my mind the memory of that kinesthetic pattern. It is evident that all manual skills depend on kinesthetic patterns, and in no art is this more important than in calligraphy. In writing, kinesthesia is specifically concerned with the visible and invisible path traced by the hand holding the writing tool: stroke sequences and directions, the visuo-muscular memory and patterns of letter parts about to be written. In calligraphy, as in other motor skills, a kinesthetic pattern is characterized by its original motions; obviously the hand can make certain strokes more easily than others. For example, by a right-hander a diagonal stroke from upper right to lower left is more comfortably and easily made than a vertical or horizontal one, a curved than a straight one, and a tilted oval than a true circle. This explains why a right-hander's informal cursive writing tends to slant to the right.[18]

From Rudolf Steiner we know of the four "will senses" (touch, life, self-movement, and balance) and their interconnections with the four "mind senses" (hearing, language, thought, and awareness of the other person—I and you, the sense of ego).[19] These four will senses are at the service of the soul long before the sight and hearing senses come under control. A mother immediately distinguishes when a baby's cry is a hungry one—the sense of vitality (sense of life) has warned the baby of the ebbing of his life forces—or when it comes from a constriction to his desired movement or need. When newborn, the condition of the body is the soul's objective outer world, and the deeply embedded senses of touch, life, self-movement, and balance tell the baby about his body. If the child is not allowed to develop at his own pace, if he does not have enough practice at sucking when feeding from breast or bottle, but is too early spoon fed, for example, and/or helped to walk too soon, then the integration of these senses and the response of his will to the impressions from these four senses are weakened. Not only does this have a weakening effect on the sense organs themselves, but the effects go far deeper, because these will senses become foundations for those which we use to communicate with our fellow human beings. The senses of hearing, language, thought, and awareness of the other person (sense of ego) are at risk.

When our students do not feel the difference between the sounds of speech, cannot distinguish cup from cap, when they cannot grasp our explanations, when their speaking is slovenly, the sounds not properly articulated, then the foundational senses of balance, vitality (life), and self-movement have been weakened. With this knowledge we can see how all that Rudolf Steiner has given in his pedagogical methods has a healing and reviving effect on these all-important bodily (will) senses that inform us of the creative powers of that universal life of which we are a part.

Exercises and Activities to Support the Struggling Child

Steiner emphasizes that teachers must work at their own speech so that it becomes objective and not embedded in habit patterns and tones.[20] He gave specific speech exercises in the first training course for Waldorf school teachers; he expected them to practice eurythmy and painting, too. These subjects are a powerful means of reviving the intimate connections between hearing, self-movement, and language. Painting is a reviver of the sense of vitality (foundation for the sense of thought), as also is the making of riddles, which are given in the curriculum of the first three grades. These activities thus stimulate the metamorphosis of the sense of life into the concept or thought sense.[21]

Symmetry form drawings and dexterity exercises work towards establishing the child's relationship to the sense of balance. Dexterity exercises might include body geography exercises,[22] jumping rope and Chinese jump rope, drawing a figure 8 in the air with the dominant hand and then with the nose, tracing circles in the air with each hand moving in opposite directions. This sense of balance is the foundation for the sense of hearing. It prepares him to hear the melody, harmony, and rhythms of music, movement, and speech.

These exercises are the great healers for the stresses and gaps in the development of early childhood. The longterm effects of these healing activities should never be underrated. What we have done for the children does not end when they leave school. Our pedagogy will continue to work in the subconscious regions of the soul, and the fruits will appear long after the means have faded from the memory.

Bad writing postures can be cured by giving the student a suitable imagination (see chapter 3). We can help an older child by letting him stand and write at the blackboard for a short time each day. If bad habits are too firmly ingrained we could try using a drawing board at an angle of 45 degrees to support his writing and drawing. When the eye is thus directed at 90 degrees onto the paper, the sense of self-movement is freshly stimulated. Ideally all writing should be done on a sloping surface. Until the end of World War II, school desks were supplied with sloping tops, but nowadays this would have to be scientifically reevaluated in order to reappear.

We should notice when a child leans forward and curves the non-writing arm around the top of the paper or book as he writes, or supports his head with this hand—a signal that there is a remaining immature movement pattern (see pages 93–95). We can assist the remedial work he is receiving by giving him a ball to hold. The hand holding the ball should be cupped with its back resting on the desk. Ideally the ball would be made of copper, a metal which warms itself from the heat of the body and stimulates the circulation, but one firmly stuffed with sheep's wool could be a substitute. If neither is possible, then an orange can serve our purpose.

The Left-Handed Child

The subject of left-handedness could fill a book. My observation and experience of the various types of left-handedness has been corroborated by the research of William Gaddes at the University of British Columbia, Vancouver, B.C., Canada, in 1985.[23]

The main causes of left-handedness are:

- Subtle injuries in the structural (skeleton, muscles, tendons, ligaments, joints) or nervous system;

- Unresolved ambidextrousness;

- True left-handedness, i.e, decided preference for the total dominance of the left side of the body.

It is important for all children to be assessed when entering school; this assessment includes an evaluation of the child's dominance pattern.

The policy in Waldorf education, broadly speaking, has been that all children acquire, before the age of nine years, the skill of handwriting using their right hand.

Writing by hand involves two activities, the actual movements of the hand writing the letters and the thought content of the writer. For writing to proceed smoothly, the former has to be subservient to the latter and not impinge on consciousness.

Today we are aware of the specialized function of the brain hemispheres. The left hemisphere which is activated with the right side of the body, deals mainly with verbalization, speech, and the intellectual-cognitive language-related faculties. The right hemisphere, which is activated by the left side of the body, deals mainly with the artistic, the imagination, and with spatial elements. A dynamic concept of brain function is now accepted; the hemispheres and the rest of the brain work as a unit.[24]

We damp down and constrain the natural functioning of the right hemisphere if we impose on it the monitoring of the intellectual language activity of composing writing, by writing with the left hand. Research has shown that speech disturbances are not caused by changing the handedness skill of either left- or right-handed children.[25] A person's right hand can be taught a skill when there is a left-sided dominance, just as a left hand can acquire a skill with a right-sided dominance.

The decision to teach the right hand of a left-hander the skill of handwriting is one which depends on the constitution of the child. This is a medical question and is best decided, after the appropriate neurological assessments, by the school doctor (or an anthroposophical doctor in the community) with the parents and the teacher giving their input.[26] When available, a doctor will prescribe the appropriate exercises for the therapeutic eurythmist to carry out. In the classroom the teacher must also make allowances for the speed of handwriting and the quality of work expected from the child during this time of learning a new skill.

The left-handed children who are to use the right hand for the skill of handwriting continue to use the dominant left hand and side of the body for all other activities—painting, drawing, handwork and games. Needless to say, the accomplishment that can be helpful for all degrees of left-handedness is piano playing.

A child who comes later into the Waldorf school, who is already settled into left handwriting needs to be carefully observed to see how he sits. To avoid smudging his writing as he moves his hand, the paper can be tilted so that the top left corner is higher than the right. The left-handed writer should keep his relaxed left upper arm comfortably near his body as he writes, keeping his shoulder down and using his fingers to make the writing movements rather than the hand and forearm. He can practice this skill by holding a marble between his left thumb and first two fingers as he would his pen and make the letter forms with the marble he is holding. Another good skill-making exercise is to spin a little finger top. The function of the right hand is to move the page up towards the top of the desk as the writing proceeds. A left-handed child needs to sit to the left of a right-handed child to avoid their arms colliding as they write and draw.

Aids to Continue Good Handwriting

Throughout the years of school, to prevent the deterioration of handwriting through the hurried taking of notes and dictation, time should be given, once in each main lesson block, to the enjoyment of writing beautifully. This would give teachers an opportunity to make the children conscious of the necessity for correct management of pens, paper, and their sitting positions. In the high school, the discipline of making the correct movement sequences of the letters with a broad-nibbed pen has a quieting effect, similar to that of geometry, on the turbulent forces of puberty. In writing thus, young people can experience a musical element which complements the spatial "speech" of geometry. Needless to say, some good examples by the teacher would be a great stimulus to this, just as examples of paintings which are made by the teachers for the classrooms of the lower school at the seasonal festivals, or for birthdays, are a help in encouraging the younger children in their painting.

In spite of having had many daily opportunities for finger activities, some children still end up having poor finger skills. They may have had birth or whiplash traumas to the neck and/or head areas; as the nerves in the muscles of the arm and hand are connected to the neck these often subtle traumas can nevertheless become the source of awkward fine motor skills. These children benefit from an evaluation and treatment of their structural physical status.[27]

A practical remedial activity as a corrective to stiff wrists and tightly held pencils is for children to make large capital letters in the shaded drawing technique. This will help to overcome the automatic movements that so easily become habit as children begin to develop speed in writing. Other exercises to help release tension in arms and hands are described in *The Extra Lesson*, chapter 5, pages 140–141. A comfortable and supportive rubber pencil grip which fits both right- and left-handed writers is now available for use by students who grasp their pencils in tense or awkward ways.[28]

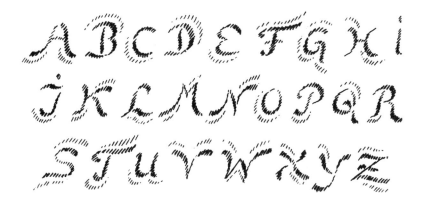

We should be alert to other aspects of poor handwriting which can be caused by fatigue, allergies, or emotional problems. The first two are likely to produce different standards of hand-written work during a week or even in a day in the case of allergies, varying according to what has been eaten or according to the seasonal air quality changes. Emotional problems often reveal themselves by a mixture of handwriting styles in the same written passage whether it has been copied, written from dictation, or is the child's own composition.

Today's mainstream answer for children struggling with handwriting is often to place them at the computer early on. This by-passes an essential process, the development and integration of the child's capacities through the effort of overcoming obstacles with the support and guidance of caring adults. It is also important to note that the way the hands are used is reflected in the development of the brain.[29]

In conclusion, if we use the methods that belong to the essential development of human beings as spiritual beings, we place in them a seed instead of a stone. In due course, this will receive water from some other teacher, perhaps a long time after. Then the seed will germinate, and in a few weeks the student will master, through the power of his own will, what has been hampering him.

We have to have the confidence that faculties develop when they are rightly prepared. If we do this conscientiously, we are giving our students bread from the loaf that always renews itself and water from the bottle that is never empty.

As Rudolf Steiner said, "Pedagogy is love for the human being resulting from knowledge of the human being, and this is the bringing of the living spirit right down into the bodily constitution, the bodily functions."[30]

Practical Applications and Summary

- Study the archetypal physical body in relation to neuropsychology. (See Bibliography)

- Recognize retained early movement responses (primal reflexes) and the vertical midline barrier, which interfere with handwriting. For professional diagnosis and remediation see note 13.

- Remember the transformation of the four will (movement) senses into the four mind (thinking) senses, and factors inhibiting this process.[31]

- Exercises for individuals with concentration difficulties and for restless classes are:

  1. For individual children: painting exercises and creating riddles;

  2. Before the morning verse, have the students do ten minutes of movement and speech exercises: walking, clapping to music or speech, clapping and stamping exercises (also with eyes closed to awaken listening), hopping, skipping, and movement concentration exercises, recitation of tables with movement (stepping, stamping, skipping, jumping forward and back);

  3. Alternate these movement exercises with a color painting exercise especially on Monday mornings.[32]

- Form drawing, including forms in shaded drawing and painting forms; symmetry exercises are good for left-right issues.[33]

- For reversal problems: all the spatial dimensions are contained in the spiral. The soul faculties corresponding to these spatial dimensions are brought into activity when drawing this form (see Chapter 3). Have the child say the directions, as indicated below, while he draws each large form.

A

Clockwise: begin to the left, then up to the right, down, up and around to counter-clockwise.

B

Counter-clockwise: to the left, down, right, up, left, down and around to clockwise.

Clockwise: to the right, down, left, up, right, down, up and around to counter-clockwise.

Counter-clockwise: to the right, up, left, down, right, up, left, down and around to clockwise.

- As the basic neurology of skills necessary for handwriting engender and support the faculty of reading, make sure these skills are covered. Learn the symptoms showing a lack of such skills.

- For children who hold the pencil/pen in tense and/or awkward ways, use the pencil grips mentioned in this chapter.

- Look at the suggestions for remediation in the classroom; individual assessment and support is needed when classroom work does not lead to sufficient improvement.[34]

- Reasons for lack of coordination, lack of handedness skills, and for ambidextrousness are covered in this chapter; dominance and laterality are defined.

- Study the students' postures: correction of bad habits is important.

- For the left-handed writers, there are specific aids to posture and handwriting.

- The discipline of correct letter formation must be maintained through vigilant observation and practice. See illustration **p 56**.

- In sixth grade:

  1. If not yet done: introduce a specific book for the careful writing of poems and quotations.

  2. Use shaded capital letters to correct tight pencil holds, mechanical writing movements, and/or tense wrists. The Roman and medieval history main lesson blocks give us the opportunity to do this. (The students may also write with dipping pens for experiencing the slow and careful writing of the monks.)

3. Teachers, remember to distinguish between the need for speed and the using of one's best handwriting. Once a week the children practice their best handwriting, bringing attention back to the letter formation, paper and sitting position, pencil/pen hold, etc., as it is now that the children tend to establish their own individual style of handwriting. We should not disturb this development by introducing stylized hands such as italic script. Occasional inspection and criticism of the student's work only damages the children's will development. As always, it is important to praise good work.

Biographies

Some of the authors who are referred to in this book have made very significant contributions to our knowledge about the development of writing and its place in human consciousness. Some brief details on major characters are given below.

Catich, Edward M. [1906–1979]
Edward Catich was a calligrapher, topographer, and lecturer at St. Ambrose College in Davenport, Iowa. He was one of the leaders of the calligraphy movement in the United States, stimulated by the work of Edward Johnston. Catich's book *The Origin of the Serif: Brush Writing and Roman Letters* is now a classic and contains, in brush strokes, the capital letters which can be seen on the Trajan Column in Rome. These are printed in terra cotta, the color used for the tiles of the Roman baths. They are on separate sheets, because he wished them to be viewed from the vertical distance in space as they would be seen on the triumphal column. This book is available at the library of California State University Sacramento, but may not be taken away from the library. Catich was also editor of Catfish Press in Iowa.

Diringer, David, M.A. (Cantab.), D.Litt. (Florence) [1900–1975]
David Diringer was educated in Florence, Italy, and returned to the university there as a lecturer, then as a professor. He had many appointments which included lecturer in Semitic Epigraphy at Cambridge and secretary of the Permanent Committee of Etruscan Studies. Dr. Diringer was the founder and director of the Alphabet Museum at Cambridge, one of the finest such collections in its time. After his death it was transferred to the University of Tel Aviv.

Fairbank, Alfred, C.B.E. [1895–1982]

Alfred Fairbank combined calligraphy with his profession as a senior executive officer of the Admirality. He served as president of the Society of Scribes and Illuminators from 1951 to 1963. He was a member of the Society of Designer Craftsmen and received the Leverhulme Research Award twice. He was also vice president of the Society of Italic Handwriting, and he designed and had responsibility for the Books of Remembrance of the Royal Air Force at the Church of St. Clement Danes.

Johnston, Edward [1872–1944]

Edward Johnston gave the major impetus for the revival of formal calligraphy, and his teaching created the International School of Scribes. In 1906 he wrote *Writing, Illuminating, and Lettering*, a title which has never been superseded. He reconstructed medieval techniques of pen cutting and velum preparation. His foundational hand has been the starting point of the modern development in calligraphy, and he trained most of the founder members of the Society of Scribes and Illuminators.

Johnston held that, in all work, truth must be sought and that the main approach to this was through religion, science, and art. He indicated that the thought which inspires his work has been to make living letters with a formal pen. One of Johnston's most enduring works was the creation of the lettering used by the London Underground which has not been superseded for its clarity and beauty.

Kellogg, Rhoda [1898–   ]

Mrs. Rhoda Kellogg, a preschool educator since 1928, held a bachelor's degree from the University of Minnesota and a master's degree from Columbia University; she had educational work experience in New Jersey, New York, and California.

Her interest in children's drawings was inspired by the work of Austrian art teacher Franz Cizek. He was the first teacher to consider children's early drawings as an art form in its own right. Mrs. Kellogg worked at the Phoebe Hearst Golden Gate Preschool Learning Center in San Francisco, California. This school is one of the remaining of a network of kindergartens, founded in 1895 with the financial support of prominent San Franciscans. During the time she worked there, no fees were charged, attendance was entirely voluntary, and children could come and go as they pleased. The school therefore received children of all ethnic and cultural backgrounds directly from the surrounding neighborhoods.

It was from her time at Phoebe Hearst that she built up a collection of half a million children's drawings, tracing the artistic development of children from two to eight years of age. She traveled widely, lecturing to students and professionals working with children. During her travels, she added examples of drawings from children in Europe and countries of the Near and Far East; she received 5,000 drawings from thirty countries.

Among her many publications, her two seminal books are *What Children Scribble and Why*, published in 1955, and *Analyzing Children's Art*, published in 1970. The Rhoda Kellogg Art Collection is now at the Appalachian State University, Boone, North Carolina, where microfiche cards of some 8,000 drawings are available to researchers.

Lethaby, William R. [1857–1931]

William Lethaby was an architect and scholar. He worked with Norman Shaw from 1879 to 1891. In 1896, he was appointed first principal of the London County Council Central School of Art. In 1900, he became professor of design at the Royal College of Art and, in 1906, surveyor to the fabric of Westminster Abbey, a post he held for 21 years.

Steiner, Rudolf [1861–1925]

Rudolf Steiner was a teacher, philosopher, writer, and lecturer. He founded the Anthroposophical Society, which embodies the teachings from his spiritual scientific research.

As a philosopher, Steiner recognized that thinking was the one faculty of the human soul that could observe its own activity using the very faculty which carries out the thinking function. In his book *Philosophy of Spiritual Activity,* he defines thinking and observation as the two faculties which, if disciplined by training, can recognize the reality that we are surrounded by an objective spiritual world. The subtitle he gave to this seminal book is: "Fundamentals of a Modern World View, Results of Introspective Observation according to the Method of Natural Science."

Based on such training he found that the life of Jesus Christ, His Death, and Resurrection had given meaning to the evolution of the cosmos and humanity, when recognized as an organization evolving from the activities of spiritual beings. This may briefly be summarized as follows:

Steiner explains, from his spiritual insight, how the organ of the human being's I-consciousness—the physical body—has, since the Fall, united itself more and more with the chemical substances the human being assimilates from the earth. The spiritual archetypal body, created for us by the spiritual beings concerned with our evolution, had become so defined by the substances consumed during incarnation in a physical body that its existence was in danger of dissolution along with the physical matter of the body when it decayed at death.

Christ rescued for humankind the spiritual archetype of the physical body, the organ which reflects back to us our I, which is the eternal member of the human organization. Christ now lives in this perfected, resurrected, spiritual archetype of the physical body, and works from within the spiritual atmosphere of the earth. Rudolf Steiner spoke of this in lectures published as *The Gospel of St. John in Relation to the Other Gospels*. Christ's statement, "Lo, I am with you always, even unto the end of the world." (Matt. 28:20) embodies this actuality.

Therefore those human souls who unite themselves with His aims for humankind will also wish to return ever again to the place where He is working for the brotherhood of humanity and for the spiritualization of the Earth. This Christianized concept of reincarnation and human evolution is the inspiration for the practical work which embraces education, medical research, curative education, agriculture, and economics. In the arts, Steiner established his own original contribution with the formation of eurythmy. The present Goetheanum in Dornach, Switzerland, was the second of two buildings which he designed as the headquarters of the Anthroposophical Society. There are now national societies in nearly every European country, North, Central, and South America, as well as in Asia, Australia, New Zealand, and South Africa and other countries in Africa.

Steiner's impulse for architecture has given the impetus for the design of school buildings; this one is Stegmann Hall at Rudolf Steiner College, Fair Oaks, California.

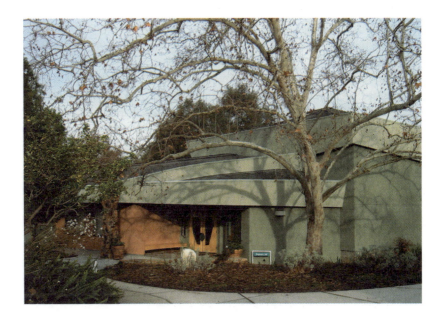

References and Notes

Chapter 1: The Relationship of the Three Dimensions of Space to the Growing Child

1. Kellogg, Rhoda, *Analyzing Children's Art*, 262-263.

2. Steiner, Rudolf, *The Renewal of Education*, Lecture 6.

3. Steiner, Rudolf, *The Education of the Child*, Part I.

4. Critchlow, Keith and Jon Allen, *The Whole Question of Health: An Inquiry into Architectural First Principles in the Designing of Healthcare Buildings*, 13-14, 18.

5. Steiner, *The Education of the Child*.

6. Steiner, *The Kingdom of Childhood* and *The Education of the Child*.

7. Greenfield, Susan, *The Human Brain: A Guided Tour*, 5-6, 110.

8. Ibid., Chapter 1.

9. Ibid., 114-115.

10. McAllen, Audrey, *The Extra Lesson*, Chapters 1, 12.

11. Critchlow and Allen, *The Whole Question of Health*.

12. Steiner, *The Education of the Child*.

Chapter 2: The Alphabet and Writing as a Picture of the Development of Human Consciousness

1. Diringer, David, *Writing: A Study of its Historical Evolution*.

2. Greenfield, *The Human Brain*.

3. Ibid., 36, 108-111.

4. Baring, Anne and Jules Cashford, *The Myth of the Goddess: Evolution of an Image*, 434-438, 676, 681, 664-665; and McAllen, *Sleep*.

5. Greenfield, *The Human Brain*, 146: "Memory is more than the mere function of the brain as it encapsulates individuals' inner resources for interpreting in an exquisitely unique fashion the world around them." Greenfield, *The Human Brain*, 104-115, 175-177; and Abram, David, *The Spell of the Sensuous*, 104-115, 175-177.

6. Diringer, *Writing*; Hancock, Graham, *Fingerprints of the Gods*, 104-105, 135.

7. *The Book of Kells*, ed. Peter Brown; and Abram, *The Spell of the Sensuous*, 97-101, 131-135.

8. Diringer, *The Alphabet: A Key to the History of Mankind*, 97-101, 131-135.

9. Ibid., example 134.

10. Diringer, *Writing*; Abram, *The Spell of the Sensuous*, 9, 101-102, 251-254 (and 257 for the effect of phonetic writing). Abram suggests that it was the purely phonetic Greek alphabet that abstracted human beings from their connection with the living world around them and lead to present day abstract thinking.

11. Greenfield, *The Human Brain*, 34-36.

12. Essay from *Anthroposophy*, Christmas, 1927: Gotthold E. Lessing (1729-1781), "The Education of the Human Race."

13. Steiner, *From Jesus to Christ*.

14. Bowman, Carol, *Children's Past Lives: How Past Life Memories Affect Your Child*; Abram, *The Spell of the Sensuous*, 264-265 on making "sense" of the world in which we live; and Rawson, Martyn, "Writing and Cultural Memory" in *Steiner Education*, Vol. 32, No. 2, which gives examples of application in the classroom.

15. Perry, Bruce D., M.D., Ph.D., "Memories of Fear" article available on website http://www.bcm.tmc.edu/civitas. Dr. Perry, research professor at Baylor College of Medicine and chief of psychiatry at Texas Children's Hospital, both in Houston, Texas, is the author of *Maltreated Children: Experience, Brain Development and the Next Generation* to be published by W. W. Norton & Co. His neuroscience research and practice have focused on traumatized children, examining the neuro-physiology and long-term effects of traumatic life events.

Chapter 3:   The Preparation for Writing

1. Steiner, *The Renewal of Education*, Lecture 5.

2. Steiner, in *The Child's Changing Consciousness as the Basis of Pedagogical Practice*: "It may seem very strange that writing should come before reading, but what ultimately matters is to start, not from materialistic conceptions of life and so form a preconceived idea of what the child ought to know when he is eight years old, but to know what are the consequences of this early knowledge. Too early reading directs the thoughts along abstract lines. It leads the child away from actual life. Ultimately it produces arterial sclerosis. It is always so that the influences of education on the spirit and soul of the child extend into the region of the physical in later life. To this we can add today the number of young people so under academic stress that they burn out in the early years at university." Readers, please note that this was originally written in 1923!

3. Kutzli, Rudolf, *Creative Form Drawing*, Workbooks 1, 2, 3; Embry-Stine, Laura and Ernst Schuberth, *Form Drawing for Grades One through Four*.

4. Steiner, *A Psychology of Body, Soul, and Spirit*, Part 1 Anthroposophy.

5. Kepler, Johannes, *Harmonicus Mundi*; Frohlich and Niederhauser, *Form Drawing*, 1.

6. Frohlich and Niederhauser, *Form Drawing*.

7. McAllen, *The Extra Lesson*, Chapter 5, 141.

8. Steiner, *The Spiritual Ground of Education*.

Chapter 4: Teaching the Letters as Pictures

1. Steiner, *The Renewal of Education*, Lecture 5.

2. Ibid., Lecture 10.

3. Steiner, *The Spiritual Ground of Education*, Lecture 5.

4. These cave paintings in France were discovered in 1940. They are dated approximately 20,000 B.C. and are illustrated in *The Myth of the Goddess* by Anne Baring and Jules Cashford, together with chevron patterns, wave patterns, and triangles scratched on bone from areas as far apart as the Ukraine and Siberia.

5. Steiner, Rudolf, *The Invisible Man within Us: The Pathology Underlying Therapy*.

6. Kellogg, *Analyzing Children's Art*, 262-265.

7. Steiner, *Practical Advice to Teachers*, Lecture 5.

8. Steiner, *The Renewal of Education*, Lecture 5. These lectures were given in 1920 in Basel, Swizerland, at the newly opened Waldorf School. See also the forthcoming book *Joyful Recognition* by Else Göttgens.

9. Steiner, *The Renewal of Education*, Lecture 10.

10. Steiner, *Practical Advice to Teachers*, Lecture 5.

11. Kipling, Rudyard, *Just So Stories*, Chapter 5.

12. Steiner, *Faculty Meetings with Rudolf Steiner*, meeting of 14 June, 1920; and *The Kingdom of Childhood*, Lecture 5.

13. Eurythmy is a new art of movement accompanying speech and/or music; it was inaugurated by Rudolf Steiner.

14. Steiner, *Man: Hieroglyph of the Universe* and *A Psychology of Body, Soul, and Spirit*, Part 1.

15. See Chapters 1, 3; *Learning Difficulties: A Guide for Teachers*, ed. Mary EllenWillby, Section V; McAllen, *The Extra Lesson*.

16. Greenfield, *The Human Brain*, Chapter 2, 34.

17. Lethaby, William R., "Writing and Civilization," foreword to the catalogue for exhibition of the Society of Scribes and Illuminators.

18. Steiner, *Practical Advice to Teachers*.

19. Ibid., Lecture 10.

20. Steiner, *Human Values in Education*, Lecture 3 and *The Spiritual Ground of Education*, Lecture 8.

21. Steiner, *Practical Advice to Teachers*, Lecture 4.

22. Ibid., Lecture 5.

Chapter 5:   Reading Your Own Handwriting

1. Steiner, *The Kingdom of Childhood*.

2. Ibid., Lecture 4; Sanders, Barry, *A is for Ox*.

3. Sanders, *A is for Ox*; Honeyford, R., "Class Talk" in *The British Journal of Disorders of Communication*, Vol. 7, No. 2, 1972.

4. Göttgens, *Joyful Recognition*. This book describes the Waldorf way to teach reading.

5. Steiner, *The Kingdom of Childhood*.

6. Gaddes, William, *Learning Disabilities and Brain Function*, 226-228.

7. Johnston, Edward, *Writing, Illuminating and Lettering*.

8. Fairbank, Alfred, Charlotte Stone and Winifred Hooper, *The Story of Handwriting: A Handwriting Manual*.

9. Kellogg, *Analyzing Children's Art*, 262.

10. Sassoon, Rosemary, *Handwriting: A New Perspective*, 8.

11. Frohlich and Niederhauser, *Form Drawing*.

12. Kellogg, *Analyzing Children's Art*.

13. Steiner, *Faculty Meetings with Rudolf Steiner*, Meeting of 28 October, 1922 and *Practical Advice to Teachers*.

14. Nezoes, Renna, *Interpretation of Handwriting*; Willby, *Learning Difficulties*, Section VI, "Teachers, Look to Your Handwriting."

15. Johnston, *Writing, Illuminating and Lettering*.

16. Greenfield, The Human Brain, Chapter 2, 36, 37: "Dexterity with our hand distinguishes primates from all other animals . . . the more precise the movements generated, the larger the area of the brain is devoted to them." Page 39: "Imagine, for example, that you have to trace a complex pattern onto paper. Your hand is under constant surveillance from your eyes." See also ref. 13 and Wilson, Frank, *The Hand: How Its Use Shapes the Brain, Language, and Human Culture*.

17. Lyra colored pencils from Germany are available from Waldorf school shops, art shops, or shops stocking publications related to Waldorf/Steiner education.

18. Steiner, *A Modern Art of Education*, Lecture 8; these lectures were given in Ilkley, UK, in August, 1923.

19. Johnston, *Writing, Illuminating and Lettering*.

20. Steiner, *The Renewal of Education*, Lecture 8. In this lecture, page 102, Steiner says, "In the ninth year, as a result of important changes in soul and body, the child's character

undergoes a complete transformation. Feeling himself as a separate entity from his surroundings, he now learns to discriminate between his own selfhood and the outer world. If we observe rightly, we will see that before this change of consciousness occurs, outer world and inner experience more or less flow together. But approximately from the ninth year onward the child begins to distinguish between his own inner self and the external world. We must bear this in mind when preparing our lessons and deciding what teaching methods to use in the case of children aged nine plus. Before that time it is far better not to confuse them with descriptions of happenings in outer nature which have their own separate existence and which need to be considered objectively. Therefore, when telling fables or fairy tales we speak about animals and even plants as if they too, were human. We personify them simply because the child at that stage cannot yet distinguish between self and the world." Also, Baring and Cashford, *The Myth of the Goddess*, page 435 has a description of humanity's earliest consciousness of a living empathy with nature; modern consciousness is described on page 676.

21. These rubber pencil grips (in various colors from very bright neon colors to classic red and navy; make sure to specify) are available in small or bulk quantities from: Pencil Grips, P.O. Box 67096, Los Angeles, CA 90067.

22. Nash-Wortham, Mary, *Phonic Rhyme Time*.

23. Catich, Edward M., *The Origin of the Serif: Reed, Pen and Brush Alphabets for Writing and Lettering*.

24. Frohlich and Niederhäuser, *Form Drawing*.

25. Pink books are available from Mercurius, Fabrieksweg 1, 5683PN Best, Holland or from Mercurius School Supplies, 7426 Sunset Avenue, Fair Oaks, CA 95628 (Tel 916-863-0411, FAX 916-863-5308).

26. Ellis, Irene and Audrey McAllen, "Teachers, Look to Your Handwriting" in *Learning Difficulties*.

27. Steiner, *Lectures to Teachers*, given in Dornach, Switzerland, Christmas, 1921, report by Albert Steffen.

Chapter 6:   Oh, Spelling!

1. Steiner, *Practical Advice to Teachers*, Lecture 5.

2. Steiner, *The Education of the Child*, Part I and König, Karl, *The First Three Years of the Child*.

3. Clairborne, Robert, *English: Its Life and Times*; Barfield, Owen, *History in English Words*; Gordon, Ian, *Take My Word for It: The Riddles of English Usage*.

4. Steiner, *Discussions with Teachers*, Lectures 5-15.

5. Sanders, *A is for Ox*.

6. Nash-Wortham, *Phonic Rhyme Time* and *Take Time*, 35-37.

7. Steiner, *Education for Adolescents*, Lecture 3.

8. Dr. Samuel Johnson (1709-1784), English lexicographer, published the massive two-volume dictionary that regularized English spelling. It remained authoritative for over a century and is still remarkable for the vision of its definitions.

9. Steiner, *Man as a Being of Sense and Perception* ; Soesman, Albert, *Our Twelve Senses*; Aeppli, Willi, *The Care and Development of the Human Senses*.

10. Steiner, *The Spiritual Ground of Education* and *The Kingdom of Childhood*.

11. McAllen, *The Listening Ear*; Nash-Wortham, *Value Your Voice*.

12. *The Oxford Spelling Dictionary*; Schonell, Fred J., *Essentials in Teaching and Testing Spelling*; Dolch, *Sight Word Activities* (Spectrum Series); Phenix, Jo, *Spelling Teachers Book of Lists*; Terban, Marvin and Harry Campbell, *The Scholastic Dictionary of Spelling: Over 15,000 Words*; Vos Savant, Marilyn, *The Art of Spelling: The Method and the Madness*.

13. Rainbow notebooks are available from Rainbow Spelling Books, 1102 Raymond Street, Bellingham, WA 98226.

14. Aitken, Gillian, *Spotlight on Words* and *Spotlight on Blends*, Books I and II.

15. Steiner, *The Kingdom of Childhood*.

16. McAllen, *The Extra Lesson*.

17. Steiner, *Man: Hieroglyph of the Universe*.

Chapter 7:   Writing Difficulties

1. Steiner, Rudolf, *The Foundations of Human Experience*, also published in the translation entitled *The Study of Man*.

2. Steiner, *The Spiritual Ground of Education*.

3. de Quiros, Julio and Orlando Schrager, *Neuro-Psychological Fundamentals of Learning Disabilities*; *Learning Difficulties*, Section I, "The Postural System."

4. Husemann, Armin, *The Harmony of the Human Body*.

5. Critchlow and Allen, *The Whole Question of Health*.

6. Sir Charles Scott Sherrington (1857-1952), British scientist and physician, laid the foundations for neuropsychology. His research and publications deal principally with the brain and the nervous system. He was awarded the Nobel Prize for Medicine in 1932.

7. Strauss, *Understanding Children's Drawings*; Kellogg, *Analyzing Children's Art*.

8. Goddard, Sally, *A Teacher's Window into the Child's Mind*.

9. Field, Jane, *A Vicious Circle*.

10. Ayres, Jean, *Sensory Integration and the Child*; Kranowitz, Carol, *The Out-of-Sync Child: Recognizing and Coping with Sensory Integration Dysfunction*; Holle, Britta, *Motor Development in Children*.

11. Field, *Talking to Teachers* and *Accommodating the Neuro-Developmentally Delayed Child within the Classroom*; Goddard, *A Teacher's Window into the Child's Mind*.

12. Field, *Your Vision is Perfect: Why Don't You See?*; Goddard, *A Teacher's Window into the Child's Mind*.

13. Ibid.; Willby, *Learning Difficulties*, Section II, 60-65. For diagnosis and remediation of immature movement patterns caused by retained primal reflexes, contact an occupational or physical therapist (particularly someone working with the pediatric population using Sensory Integration) or a neuro-developmental therapist. Traditional childhood games and activities, for example, jumping rope, playing with marbles, swinging, tying knots, sweeping, modeling with plasticine or beeswax, paperfolding, all support the development of more mature movements.

14. McAllen, *The Extra Lesson*, Chapter Five, 158-174; Willby, *Learning Difficulties*, Section V, 193-194.

15. Paley, Vivian Gussin, *You Can't Say, You Can't Play*.

16. Steiner, *Practical Advice to Teachers*.

17. *Learning Difficulties*, Section II, 66-74; McAllen, *The Extra Lesson*.

18. Catich, Edward, *The Origin of the Serif*.

19. Steiner, *Man as a Being of Sense and Perception*; Aeppli, *The Care and Development of the Human Senses*; Soessman, *Our Twelve Senses*; McAllen, *The Extra Lesson*; *Learning Difficulties*.

20. Steiner, *Discussions with Teachers*, Lectures 5-15; McAllen, *The Listening Ear*.

21. Steiner, *The Kingdom of Childhood* and *Man as a Being of Sense and Perception*.

22. McAllen, *The Extra Lesson*; Willby, *Learning Difficulties*, Section V.

23. Gaddes, William, *Learning Disabilities and Brain Function*. This book deals with all aspects of left-handedness in Chapter 7, 246-249.

24. Greenfield, *The Human Brain*.

25. Moore, Josephine, *Neuroanatomy Simplified*; Tomatis, Alfred, *Education and Dyslexia*.

26. See section on left-handedness in *A Guide to Child Health* by Michaela Glöckler, and Wolfgang Goebbel; also article on left-handedness by M. Glöckler in *Developmental Insights*, ed. David Mitchell.

27. Hayden, Elizabeth, *Osteopathy for Children*; *Learning Difficulties*, Section II, "Osteopathy for Children."

28. These rubber pencil grips in various colors are available in small or bulk quantities from: Pencil Grips, P.O. Box 67096, Los Angeles, CA 90067.

29. Wilson, *The Hand*; Armstrong, Alison and Casement, Charles, *The Child and the Machine: How Computers Put Our Children's Education at Risk*; Healy, Jane, *Failure to Connect*.

30. Steiner, *A Modern Art of Education*.

31. Steiner, *Man as a Being of Sense and Perception*; Willby, *Learning Difficulties*, Section I, "The Postural System."

32. McAllen, *The Extra Lesson* and *Sleep*; Willby, *Learning Difficulties*.

33. Frohlich and Niederhauser, *Form Drawing*; Kützli, Creative *Form Drawing*, Workbooks 1, 2, 3; Embry-Stine and Schuberth, *Form Drawing for Grades One through Four*; Kirchner, Hermann, *Dynamic Drawing: Its Therapeutic Aspect*.

34. McAllen, *The Extra Lesson* and *Sleep*; Willby, *Learning Difficulties*.

Bibliography

Abram, David. *The Spell of the Sensuous*. New York: Vintage Books, 1996.

Aeppli, Willi. *The Care and Development of the Human Senses*. Great Britain: Steiner School Fellowship, n.d.

Aitken, Gillian. *Spotlight on Words*. Stourbridge: The Robinswood Press, 1994.
____. *Spotlight on Blends*, Books I and II. Stourbridge: The Robinswood Press, 1994.

Alston, Jean and Jane Taylor. *Handwriting Help-Line*. Manchester: Dextral Books, 1993.

Armstrong, Alison, *The Child and the Machine: How Computers Put Our Children's Education at Risk*. Beltsville, MD: Robins Lane Press, 2001.

Audette, Lou Anne and Anne Karson. *Getting it Write*. West Bloomfield, MI: The Activities Center, Inc., 1998.

Ayres, Jean. *Sensory Integration and the Child*. Los Angeles: Western Psychological Services, 1979.

Barfield, Owen. *Saving the Appearances: A Study in Idolatry*. Middletown, CT: Wesleyan University Press, 1989.
____. *History in English Words*. London: Faber and Faber, 1967.

Baring, Anne and Jules Cashford. *The Myth of the Goddess: Evolution of an Image*. London: Penguin-Arkana, 1991.

Barnes, Henry. *A Life for the Spirit: Rudolf Steiner in the Crosscurrents of Our Time*. Hudson, NY: Anthroposophic Press, 1997.

Bennett, Jill. *Learning to Read with Picture Books*. Stroud: The Thimble Press, 1991.

Bischofsberger, Norbert. *Werden Wir Wieder-Kommen? Der Reinkarnationsgedanken Westen und die Sicht der Christlichen Echatologie*. Mainz: Grünewald Verlag, 1996.

Bowman, Carol. *Children's Past Lives: How Past Life Memories Affect Your Child*. New York: Bantam Books, 1997.

Brown, Peter, ed. *The Book of Kells*. London: Thames and Hudson, 1980.

Catich, Edward. *The Origin of the Serif: Reed, Pen and Brush Alphabets for Writing and Lettering*. Davenport: Catfish Press, 1968.

Childs, Gilbert. *Rudolf Steiner: His Life and Work*. Edinburgh: Floris Books, 1995.
____. *Steiner Education in Theory and Practice*. Edinburgh: Floris Books, 1991.
____. *Education and Beyond: Steiner and the Problems of Modern Society*. Edinburgh: Floris Books, 1996.

Clairborne, Robert. *English: Its Life and Times*. London: Bloomsbury, 1990.

Clark, Margaret M. *Teaching Left-Handed Children*. London: University of London Press, 1959.

Critchlow, Keith and Jon Allen. *The Whole Question of Health: An Inquiry into Architectural First Principles in the Designing of Healthcare Buildings*. London: The Prince of Wales Institute of Architecture, 1994.

Cripps, Charles and Robin Cox. *Joining the ABC*. Wisbech: LDA, 1989.

Diringer, David. *Writing: A Study of its Historical Evolution*. London: Thames and Hudson, 1962.

____. *The Alphabet: A Key to the History of Mankind*. London: Hutchinson International, 1968.

Dolch. *Sight Word Activities*. Spectrum Series. New York: McGraw Hill, 1999.

Drummond, Richard. *A Broader Vision: Perspectives on the Buddha and the Christ*. Virginia: A.R.E., 1996.

Embry-Stine, Laura and Ernst Schuberth. *Form Drawing: Grades One through Four*. Fair Oaks, CA: Rudolf Steiner College Press, 1999.

Fairbank, Alfred with Charlotte Stone and Winifred Hooper. *The Story of Handwriting: A Handwriting Manual*. London: Ginn and Co., Beacon Writing Books, no date.

Field, Jane. *Accommodating the Neuro-Developmentally Delayed Child within the Classroom*. Wickenford, UK: Jane Field Publications, 1992.

____. *The Role of the Corpus Callosum on the Acquisition of the Three R's*. Wickenford, UK: Jane Field Publications, 1995.

____. *Talking to Teachers*. Wichenford, UK: Jane Field Publications, 1990.

____. *A Vicious Circle*. Wickenford, UK: Jane Field Publications, 1993.

____. *Your Vision is Perfect: Why Don't You See?* Wichenford, UK: Jane Field Publications, 1992.

Finser, Torin. *School as a Journey*. Hudson, NY: Anthroposophic Press, 1994.

Frohlich, Margaret and Hans Niederhauser. *Form Drawing*. Spring Valley: Mercury Press, 1974.

Frommer, Eva. *A Voyage through Childhood into the Adult World: Developmental Aspects*. Stroud: Hawthorn Press, 1994.

Gaddes, William H. *Learning Disabilities and Brain Function: A Neuro-psychological Approach*. New York: Springer Verlag, 1985.

Girdham, Arthur. *The Cathars and Reincarnation: We Are One Another*. London: Spearman, 1970.

Gladich, Joen and Paula Sassi. *The "Write" Approach*, Books 1 and 2. Fair Oaks, CA: Rudolf Steiner College Press, 1991.

Glöckler, Michaela. "Aspects of Left-handedness" in *Developmental Insights*. David Mitchell, ed. Fair Oaks, CA: Association of Waldorf Schools of North Aamerica Publications, 1997.

Glöckler, Michaela and Wolfgang Goebbel. *A Guide to Child Health*. Edinburgh: Floris Books, 1990.

Goddard, Sally. *A Teacher's Window into the Child's Mind*. Eugene, OR: Fern Ridge Press, 1997.

Goetheanum School of Spiritual Science. *Rudolf Steiner: An Illustrated Biography*. Dornach, Switzerland. London: Rudolf Steiner Press, 1972.

Gordon, Ian. *Take my Word for It: Riddles of English Usage*. Auckland: Wilson and Horton, 1997.

Göttgens, Else, *Joyful Recognition*. A forthcoming book about teaching reading.

Gray, Nicolette. *Letters as Drawing*. Oxford: Oxford University Press, 1971.

Greenfield, Susan. *The Human Brain: A Guided Tour*. New York: Basic Books, 1997.

Grimley, Ann and A. McKinlay. *The Clumsy Child*. Ilkley, U.K.: Association of Paediatric Chartered Physiotherapists, 1977.

Hancock, Graham. *Fingerprints of the Gods*. London: BCA William Heineman, 1995.

Hayden, Elizabeth. *Osteopathy for Children*. Painswick, U.K.: Viners Wood, 2000.

Healy, Jane. *Endangered Minds*. New York: Simon & Schuster, 1990.

____. *Failure to Connect: How Computers Affect our Children's Minds—for Better and Worse*. New York: Simon & Schuster, 1998.

Hemleben, Johannes. *Rudolf Steiner: A Documentary Biography*. East Grinstead, Sussex: Henry Goulden, 1975.

Holle, Britta. *Motor Development in Children*. Oxford: Blackwell Scientific Publications Ltd., 1976.

Honeyford, R. "Class Talk" in *The British Journal of Disorders of Communication*, Vol. 7, No. 2, 1972.

Husemann, Armin. *The Harmony of the Human Body.Edinburgh: Floris, 1989*.

Jarman, Christopher. *The Development of Handwriting Skills*. Oxford: Blackwell, Primary Education, 1979; paperback, Thornes, 1996.

Johnston, Edward. *Writing, Illuminating and Lettering*. London: Pitman, 1906.

Johnswood, Launcelot. *You Can Read*. Australia: Angus and Robertson, 1988.

Kellogg, Rhoda. *Analyzing Children's Art*. Mountain View, CA: Mayfield Publishing Company, 1969.

Kipling, Rudyard. *Just So Stories*. London: MacMillan, 1972. First published in 1902.

Kirchner, Hermann. *Dynamic Drawing: Its Therapeutic Aspect*. Spring Valley, NY: Mercury Press, 1977.

Kohen-Raz, Reuven. *Learning Disabilities and Postural Control*. Israel: Freund Publishing House, 1986.

König, Karl. *The First Three Years of the Child*. Hudson, NY: Anthroposophic Press, 1969.

Kranowitz, Carol. *The Out-of-Sync Child: Recognizing and Coping with Sensory Integration Dysfunction*. New York: Perigee, 1998.

Kutzli, Rudolf, *Creative Form Drawing, Work Books 1, 2* and *3*. Stroud: Hawthorn Press, 1985.

Lessing, G. "The Education of the Human Race," in *Anthroposophy*, Christmas 1927.

Lethaby, William R. "Writing and Civilization," foreword to the catalogue for an exhibition of the Society of Scribes and Illuminators.

Lievegoed, Bernard. *Phases of Childhood*. Edinburgh: Floris Books, 1997.

Lissau, Rudi. *Rudolf Steiner*. Stroud: Hawthorn Press, 1987.

McAllen, Audrey. *The Extra Lesson* (5th edition). Fair Oaks: Rudolf Steiner College Press, 1999.
____. *The Listening Ear*. Stroud: Hawthorn Press, 1989.
____. *Sleep*. Stroud: Hawthorn Press, 1995.

Mitchell, David, ed. *Developmental Insights*. Fair Oaks, CA: Association of Waldorf Schools of North America, 1997.

Moore, Josephine. *Neuroanatomy Simplified*. Dubuque, IA: Kendall Hunt, 1969.

Murray, Marcia. *Masks and Reflections in Ourselves and Our Handwriting*. Mona Vale, Australia: Eagle Publishers, 1997.

Nash-Wortham, Mary. *Phonic Rhyme Time*. Stourbridge: The Robinswood Press, 1993.
____. *Value your Voice*. Stourbridge: The Robinswood Press, 1995.

Nash-Wortham, Mary and Jean Hunt. *Take Time*. Stourbridge: Robinswood Press, 1994.

Nezos, Renna. *The Interpretation of Handwriting*. London: Rider and Co., 1986.

Olivaux, Robert. *Pédagogie de L'Ecriture et Graphothérapie*. Montreal: Masson, 1988. Chapter 8, "On the Remediation of Handwriting," translation by Joen Gladich, from Handwriting Consultants International.

The Oxford Spelling Dictionary. Oxford: Oxford University Press, 1997.

Paley, Vivian Gussin. *You Can't Say, You Can't Play*. Boston: Harvard University Press, 1993.

Paul, Diane G. *The Left-Hander's Handbook*. Stourbridge: Robinswood Press, 1998.

Phenix, Jo. *Spelling Teachers Book of Lists*. Ontario: Pembroke Pub. Ltd., 1996.

Purse, Jo. *The Mystic Spiral: Journey of the Soul*. London: Thames & Hudson, 1994.

Querido, René, ed. *A Western Approach to Reincarnation and Karma: Selected Lectures and Writings by Rudolf Steiner*. Hudson: Anthroposophic Press, 1997.

de Quiros, Julio, and Orlando Schrager. *Neuro-Psychological Fundamentals of Learning Disabilities*. Novato, CA: Academic Therapy Publications, 1988.

Rawson, Martyn. "Writing and Cultural Memory" in *Steiner Education*, Vol. 32, No. 2.

Rodgers, Vimala. *Your Handwriting Can Change Your Life*. New York: Simon and Schuster, 2000.

Salter, Joan. *The Incarnating Child*. Stroud: Hawthorn Press, 1987.

Sassoon, Rosemary. *The Art and Science of Handwriting*. London: Intellect Books, 1993.
____. *Handwriting: A New Perspective*. Cheltenham: Leopard Learning, 1990.

Sassoon, Rosemary and Pat Savage. *Handwriting: The Way to Teach It*. Cheltenham: Leopard Learning, 1990.

Sanders, Barry. *A is for Ox*. New York: Pantheon Books, 1994.

Schneider, Michael S. *A Beginner's Guide to Constructing the Universe*. New York: Harper Perennial, 1995.

Schonell, Fred J. *Essentials in Teaching and Testing Spelling*. London: MacMillan, 1951.

Schwartz, Eugene. *Rhythms and Turning Points in the Life of the Child*. Fair Oaks: Rudolf Steiner College Press, 1991.
____. *Millenial Child*. Hudson, NY: Anthroposophic Press, 1999.

Soesman, Albert. *Our Twelve Senses*. Stroud: Hawthorne Press, 1999.

Goetheanum School of Spiritual Science. *Rudolf Steiner: An Illustrated Biography*. Dornach, Switzerland. London: Rudolf Steiner Press, 1972.

Steiner, Rudolf. *Autobiography: Chapters in the Course of my Life 1861-1907*. Hudson, NY: Anthroposophic Press, 1999. GA28.
____. *The Child's Changing Consciousness as the Basis of Pedagogical Practice*. Hudson, NY: Anthroposophic Press, 1996. GA306.
____. *The Christ Impulse and Evolution of Ego-Consciousness*. Hudson, NY: Anthroposophic Press, 1991. GA116.
____. *Christianity as Mystical Fact*. Bristol: Rudolf Steiner Press, 1992 and Hudson: Anthroposophic Press, 1997. GA8.
____. *Discussions with Teachers*. Hudson, NY: Anthroposophic Press, 1997. GA295.
____. *Education for Adolescents*. Hudson, NY: Anthroposophic Press, 1996. GA302.
____. "The Education of the Child in the Light of Anthroposophy," now a section of *The Education of the Child*. Hudson, NY: Anthroposophic Press, 1996. GA34.
____. *Faculty Meetings with Rudolf Steiner*. Hudson, NY: Anthroposophic Press, 1998. GA300/a-c.

____. *The Foundations of Human Experience*. Hudson, NY: Anthroposophic Press, 1996. Formerly published in another translation under the title of *The Study of Man*. GA293.

____. *The Four Temperaments*. Hudson, NY: Anthroposophic Press, 1987. GA57.

____. *From Jesus to Christ*. London: Rudolf Steiner Press, 1991. GA 131.

____. *The Gospel of St. John in Relation to the Other Three Gospels*. New York: Anthroposophical Press, 1948.

____. *Human Values in Education*. London: Rudolf Steiner Press, 1971. Lectures given in Arnheim, the Netherlands, 1924. GA310.

____. *The Invisible Man Within Us: The Pathology Underlying Therapy*. Spring Valley, NY: Mercury Press, 1987.

____. *The Kingdom of Childhood*. London: Rudolf Steiner Press 1988 and Hudson, NY: Anthroposophic Press, 1996. Lectures given in Torquay, UK, 1924. GA311.

____. *Lectures to Teachers*. London: Rudolf Steiner Press, 1948. Dornach, Switzerland, Christmas, 1921 Report by Albert Steffen.

____. *Man: Hieroglyph of the Universe*. London: Rudolf Steiner Press, 1972. New translation, *Mystery of the Universe—The Human Being: Model of Creation*. Hudson, NY: Anthroposophic Press, 2001. GA201.

____. *Man as a Being of Sense and Perception*. North Vancouver, Canada: Steiner Book Centre, 1958. GA206.

____. *A Modern Art of Education*. London: Rudolf Steiner Press, 1981. Lectures given in Ilkley, UK, 1923. GA307.

____. *Mystery of the Universe—The Human Being: Model of Creation*. Hudson, NY: Anthroposophic Press, 2001. GA201.

____. *Philosophy, Cosmology and Religion*. Hudson, NY: Anthroposophic Press, 1984. GA215.

____. *Philosophy of Freedom*. London: Rudolf Steiner Press, 1964. Also translated as *Philosophy of Spiritual Activity*. Bristol: Rudolf Steiner Press, 1992. Newest translation: *Intuitive Thinking as a Spiritual Path*. Hudson, NY: Anthroposophic Press, 1995. GA4.

____. *Practical Advice to Teachers*. London: Rudolf Steiner Press, 1976. Lectures given in Stuttgart, Germany, 1919. GA294.

____. "Practical Training in Thinking," now a section of *Anthroposophy in Everyday Life*. Hudson: Anthroposophic Press, 1995. GA108.

____. *A Psychology of Body, Soul, and Spirit*. Hudson, NY: Anthroposophic Press, 1999. Formerly printed as *Wisdom of the Body, Soul, and Spirit: Anthroposophy, Psychosophy, Pneumatosophy*, these lectures were given in Berlin October, 1909, November, 1910, and November, 1911. GA115.

____. *The Renewal of Education*. Sussex: Steiner Schools Fellowship, 1981. Lectures given in Basel, Switzerland, 1920. GA301.

____. *Soul Economy and Waldorf Education*. London: Rudolf Steiner Press, 1986. Lectures given in Dornach, Switzerland, 1921. GA303.

____. *The Spiritual Ground of Education*. Blauvelt, NY: Garber Communications, 1989. Lectures given in Oxford, UK, 1922. GA305.

____. *Spiritual Guidance of the Individual and Humanity*. London: Rudolf Steiner Press, 1996. GA15.

Strauss, Michaela. *Understanding Children's Drawings*. London: Rudolf Steiner Press, 1988.

Taylor, Jane. "The Sequence and Structure of Handwriting Competence: Where are the Breakdown Points in the Mastery of Handwriting?" UK: Occupational Therapy, July 1985.

Terban, Marvin and Harry Campbell. *The Scholastic Dictionary of Spelling*. New York: Scholastic Reference, 2000.

Tomatis, Alfred. *Education and Dyslexia*. Fribourg, Switzerland: AIAPP, 1978.

Tseng, Mei Hui, and Sharon A. Cermak. "The Evaluation of Handwriting in Children" in *Sensory Integration Quarterly*, Volume XIX, Number 4. Los Angeles: Sensory Integration International, 1991.

Tyre, Colin and Peter Young. *Dyslexia or Illiteracy*. Milton Keynes, UK: Open University Press, 1983.

Vos Savant, Marilyn. *The Art of Spelling: The Method and the Madness*. New York: W.W. Norton & Co., 2000.

Willby, Mary Ellen. ed. *Learning Difficulties: A Guide for Teachers*, 2nd edition. Fair Oaks, CA: Rudolf Steiner College Press, 1999.

Wilson, Frank. *The Hand: How its Use Shapes the Brain, Language, and Human Culture*. New York: Pantheon Books, 1998.

References Listed by Category

The following books give an overview of Rudolf Steiner's concepts:

Rudolf Steiner. *Christianity as Mystical Fact*

_____. *From Jesus to Christ*

_____. *Man as a Being of Sense and Perception*

_____. *Philosophy, Cosmology and Religion*

_____. *Philosophy of Freedom*, also translated as *Philosophy of Spiritual Activity*

_____. "Practical Training in Thinking," in *Anthroposophy in Everyday Life*

_____. *Spiritual Guidance of the Individual and Humanity*

_____. "The Education of the Child in the Light of Anthroposophy" in *The Education of the Child*

_____. *The Four Temperaments*

_____. *A Psychology of Body, Soul, and Spirit*

_____. *The Gospel of St. John in Relation to the Other Three Gospels*

Rudolf Steiner's educational lectures referred to in this book:

Rudolf Steiner. *The Foundations of Human Experience*, also translated as *The Study of Man*

_____. *A Modern Art of Education*

_____. *Discussions with Teachers*

_____. *Faculty Meetings with Rudolf Steiner*

_____. *Education for Adolescents*

_____. *Human Values in Education*

_____. *Lectures to Teachers*

_____. *Practical Advice to Teachers*

_____. *Soul Economy and Waldorf Education*

_____. *The Child's Changing Consciousness as the Basis of Pedagogical Practice*

_____. *The Kingdom of Childhood*

_____. *The Renewal of Education*

_____. *The Spiritual Ground of Education*

Books on handwriting and reading:

Alston, Jean and Jane Taylor. *Handwriting Help-Line*

Audette, Lou Anne and Anne Karson. *Getting it Write* (a six-week therapeutic program for children experiencing handwriting difficulties)

Bennett, Jill. *Learning to Read with Picture Books*

Catich, Edward. *The Origin of the Serif: Reed, Pen and Brush Alphabets for Writing and Lettering*

Cripps, Charles and Robin Cox. *Joining the ABC*

Ellis, Irene and Audrey McAllen. "Teachers, Look to Your Handwriting" in *Learning Difficulties*, Mary Ellen Willby, ed.

Fairbank, Alfred with Charlotte Stone and Winifred Hooper. *The Story of Handwriting: A Handwriting Manual*

Gladich, Joen and Paula Sassi. *The "Write" Approach*, Books 1 and 2

Göttgens, Else. *Joyful Recognition* (a forthcoming book about teaching reading)

Jarman, Christopher. *The Development of Handwriting Skills*

Johnston, Edward. *Writing, Illuminating and Lettering*

Murray, Marcia. *Masks and Reflections in Ourselves and Our Handwriting*

Nash-Wortham, Mary. *Phonic Rhyme Time*

Nezos, Renna. *The Interpretation of Handwriting*

Rodgers, Vimala. *Your Handwriting Can Change Your Life*

Sassoon, Rosemary. *Handwriting: A New Perspective* and *The Art and Science of Handwriting*

Sassoon, Rosemary and Pat Savage. *Handwriting: The Way to Teach It*

Tyre, Colin and Peter Young. *Dyslexia or Illiteracy*

Historical aspects of writing and reading:

Baring, Anne and Jules Cashford. *The Myth of the Goddess: Evolution of an Image*

Barfield, Owen. *Saving the Appearances: A Study in Idolatry*

Brown, Peter, ed. *The Book of Kells*

Clairborne, Robert. *English: Its Life and Times*

Diringer, David. *Writing: A Study of its Historical Evolution* and *The Alphabet: a Key to the History of Mankind*

Girdham, Arthur. *The Cathars and Reincarnation: We Are One Another*

Gordon, Ian, *Take My Word For It: Riddles of English Usage*

Lessing, G. "The Education of the Human Race," essay reprinted from *Anthroposophy*, Christmas, 1927.

Sanders, Barry. *A is for Ox*

Developmental aspects of writing and reading:

Ayres, Jean. *Sensory Integration and the Child*

Clark, Margaret M. *Teaching Left-Handed Children*

Field, Jane. *A Vicious Circle, Accommodating the Neuro-Developmentally Delayed Child within the Classroom*, and *The Role of the Corpus Callosum on the Acquisition of the Three R's*

Frommer, Eva. *A Voyage through Childhood into the Adult World: Developmental Aspects*

Gaddes, William H. *Learning Disabilities and Brain Functions: A Neuro-psychological Approach*

Glöckler, Michaela, MD, and Wolfgang Goebbel, MD. *A Guide to Child Health*, chapter on left-handedness.

Greenfield, Susan. *The Human Brain: A Guided Tour*

Grimley, Ann and A. McKinlay. *The Clumsy Child*

Healy, Jane. *Endangered Minds* and *Failure to Connect: How Computers Affect our Children's Minds—for Better and Worse.*

Kellogg, Rhoda. *Analyzing Children's Art*

Kohen-Raz, Reuven. *Learning Disabilities and Postural Control*

de Quiros, Julio, MD, and Orlando Schrager, MD. *Neuro-Psychological Fundamentals of Learning Disabilities*

Moore, Josephine, OTR, PhD. *Neuroanatomy Simplified*

Mitchell, David, ed. *Developmental Insights*

Wilson, Frank. *The Hand: How Its Use Shapes the Brain, Language, and Human Culture*

Remedial aspects of writing and reading:

Gray, Nicolette. *Letters as Drawing*

Frohlich, Margaret and Hans Niederhauser. *Form Drawing*

Kirchner, Hermann. *Dynamic Drawing: Its Therapeutic Aspect*

Kützli, Rudolf. *Creative Form Drawing, Work Books 1, 2* and *3*

McAllen, Audrey. *The Extra Lesson* and *Sleep*

Olivaux, Robert. *Pedagogie de L'Ecriture et Graphothérapie*, Chapter 8, "On the Remediation of Handwriting"

Nash-Wortham, Mary and Jean Hunt. *Take Time*

Paul, Diane G. *The Left-Hander's Handbook*

Taylor, Jane, "The Sequence and Structure of Handwriting Competence: Where are the Breakdown Points in the Mastery of Handwriting?" in *Occupational Therapy*, July 1985.

Tseng, Mei Hui, MS, OTR and Sharon A. Cermak, EdD, MS, OTR. "The Evaluation of Handwriting in Children" printed in *Sensory Integration Quarterly*, Volume XIX, Number 4.

Willby, Mary Ellen, ed. *Learning Difficulties: A Guide for Teachers*

Recent books on reincarnation:

Bischofsberger, Norbert, *Werden Wir Wieder-Kommen? Der Reinkarnationsgedanken Westen und die Sicht der Christlichen Echatologie*

Bowman, Carol. *Children's Past Lives: How Past Life Memories Affect Your Child*

Drummond, Dr. Richard. *A Broader Vision: Perspectives on the Buddha and the Christ*

Querido, René, ed. *A Western Approach to Reincarnation and Karma: Selected Lectures and Writings by Rudolf Steiner*

General reading:

Aeppli, Willi. *The Care and Development of the Human Senses*

Childs, Gilbert. *Steiner Education in Theory and Practice* and *Education and Beyond: Steiner and the Problems of Modern Society*

Critchlow, Keith and Jon Allen. *The Whole Question of Health: An Inquiry into Architectural First Principles in the Designing of Healthcare Buildings*

Finser, Torin. *School as a Journey*

Hayden, Elizabeth. *Osteopathy for Children*

König, Karl. *The First Three Years of the Child*

Lievegoed, Bernard. *Phases of Childhood*

McAllen, Audrey. *The Listening Ear*

Purse, Jo. *The Mystic Spiral: Journey of the Soul*

Salter, Joan. *The Incarnating Child*

Schneider, Michael S. *A Beginner's Guide to Constructing the Universe*

Schwartz, Eugene. *Rhythms and Turning Points in the Life of the Child* and *Millenial Child*

Soesman, Albert. *Our Twelve Senses*

Strauss, Michaela. *Understanding Children's Drawings*

Biographies of Rudolf Steiner:

Barnes, Henry. *A Life for the Spirit: Rudolf Steiner in the Crosscurrents of Our Time*

Childs, Gilbert. *Rudolf Steiner: His Life and Work*

Lissau, Rudi. *Rudolf Steiner*

Hemleben, Johannes. *Rudolf Steiner: A Documentary Biography*

Rudolf Steiner, illustrated biography issued by The Goetheanum School of Spiritual Science, Dornach, Switzerland

Steiner, Rudolf. *Autobiography: Chapters in the Course of My Life, 1861-1907*

Index